PREVIOUS PAGE
A NEW WORLD

On August 24, 1992, when Hurricane Andrew hit South Florida, C. M. Guerrero was on assignment at ground zero: Florida City. Winds blasted out the bathroom wall of his motel room and buckled the ceiling. For the last 55 minutes, he was praying nonstop, crouched under a mattress. At 7:30 a.m., as the winds died down, Guerrero rushed out. The first human being he saw was Harold Keith, 69. Keith had just returned to his Florida City trailer park to find his home flattened. Keith stood in water up to his ankles, looking around, numb, trying to comprehend how this monster hurricane had so quickly destroyed everything he owned. He was holding his pants — the only possession he had left.

C.M. GUERRERO

SO LITTLE LEFT

Lazaro and Vivian Hernandez hug after finding wedding photos and a few other mementos scattered among the ruins of their mobile home near Country Walk.

BILL FRAKES

WE SHALL PREVAIL

Overnight the face of our community was transformed. So much was swept away by the fury and destruction that was Hurricane Andrew.

But Hurricane Andrew could not—can not—destroy the spirit of our community. Amidst the anguish and the pain, against great odds, the people of South Florida (and especially Dade County and Greater Miami) have shown their courage and their determination to triumph over the greatest natural disaster to befall this nation.

The Big One is a tribute to the people of this community—to those who have been hurt, and to those who have helped. Not infrequently they are the same people.

All Miami Herald profits from *The Big One*, and its companion publication in Spanish, *La Ira de los Vientos*, will go to hurricane relief efforts.

We salute the people of our community. Together, we will emerge from this stronger and more together.

Dave Lawrence

Dave Lawrence
Publisher and Chairman,
The Miami Herald/
El Nuevo Herald

SPECIAL EDITION
Waiting for the storm to arrive, a man at Hollywood Hills High shelter reads an edition of The Miami Herald that was specially distributed to shelters.
A. ENRIQUE VALENTIN

THE BIG ONE

Hurricane Andrew

Photographs by the Staffs of The Miami Herald and El Nuevo Herald

BOOK DESIGN AND EDITING BY ROMAN LYSKOWSKI AND STEVE RICE,
WITH SPECIAL ASSISTANCE FROM DENNIS COPELAND,
JOHN DORSCHNER AND CHARLES TRAINOR JR.

Andrews and McMeel
A Universal Press Syndicate Company
Kansas City

Library of Congress Cataloging-in-Publication Data

The Big One: Hurricane Andrew, photographs/by the staff of the Miami herald and el Nuevo herald; editing by Roman Lyskowski and Steve Rice, with special assistance from Dennis Copeland, John Dorschner, and Charles Trainor Jr.

p. cm.
ISBN 0-8362-8012-1 (pbk.) : $19.95
1. Hurricane Andrew, 1992—Pictorial works. 2. Hurricanes—Florida—Miami Metropolitan Area—Pictorial works. 3. Hurricanes—Florida—Dade County—Pictorial works. 4. Hurricanes—Social aspects—Florida—Miami Metropolitan Area. I. Lyskowski, Roman. II. Rice, Steve. III. Miami herald (Miami, Fla.) IV. Nuevo herald.
QC945.B54 1992
975.9'38063—dc20

92-34754
CIP

All Miami Herald profits from *The Big One*, and its companion publication in Spanish, *La Ira de los Vientos*, will go to hurricane relief efforts.

COVER PHOTOGRAPH BY TIM CHAPMAN

TITLE PAGE PHOTOGRAPH

NEW PASTIME

Determined not to let Hurricane Andrew get them down, the Castillo children — Maria, 14; D.J., 5 and Enrique, 11 — play in a Homestead yard.

A. ENRIQUE VALENTIN

CONTENTS

STANDING TALL

Nicolao Fuentes, 13, carries supplies away from a relief center at the Cutler Ridge
Mall while his father Antonio marches patriotically along.

CHARLES TRAINOR JR.

THE HURRICANE THAT

This was the storm that experts had been warning us about for years

JOHN DORSCHNER
Herald Staff Writer

Three days before Hurricane Andrew smashed into South Florida, Frank Marks was ecstatic. A veteran Miami hurricane researcher, he had been hungering for something to study, and the season had been a near-disaster for him, going well into August without a single storm worthy of a name. "I've been called pro-bad-weather," he says, slightly defensively, "but that's my business."

At first, Andrew hadn't seemed like much, a puny tropical blow that looked like it might fall apart, but then it started to strengthen. On Friday, Aug. 21, Marks eagerly raced off to Puerto Rico. Twice, he flew through the storm, measuring its complex power on his radar. He never imagined that soon he would be crammed into a two-by-four-foot bathroom with six other people and one cocker spaniel, hoping that the joy of his research wouldn't kill him and his family.

This was the Big One. Hurricane experts have been worrying about it for years: A storm with monster winds slamming into a major urban area. Casualties were remarkably light: no more than 20 in Florida were killed directly by the storm, compared to 6,000 dead from the deadliest

hurricane in U.S. history, a 1900 storm in Texas. But in terms of property destruction, Hurricane Andrew was the worst natural disaster ever to befall the United States. It changed the face of South Florida forever. Andrew destroyed $20 billion in property, demolished 25,000 homes and seriously damaged another 50,000. About 175,000 people were left homeless.

But numbers alone do not reveal the full agony and fury of the storm. What follows is a history of Hurricane Andrew, as seen through the eyes of some of those who lived through it. From an unemployed woman in a mobile home in Naranja Lakes to an affluent insurance man with a beautiful house east of Old Cutler, Andrew will be the storm they will never forget.

On Friday, Aug. 14, Frank Marks and most other experts weren't paying much attention when a wave of low-pressure air swept off West Africa. Satellite specialists at the National Hurricane Center in Coral Gables took note, but many waves come off Africa that never amount to anything. On the evening of Sunday, Aug. 16, weak winds began to circulate around the low-pressure area, and it was listed as a tropical depression. On satellite maps, it was named T.D. Three. The next day, its winds had increased to 40 mph, and the hurricane center, after an official confer-

ence, decided it was worthy of a name: Tropical Storm Andrew.

On Tuesday, the area's experts started daily 7:30 a.m. conferences at the hurricane center to keep track of Andrew, standard procedure for all tropical storms. Frank Marks, a Miami-based research meteorologist with the National Oceanic and Atmospheric Administration, and most others who attended the meetings were not initially impressed.

"The thing was kind of looking bad," Marks recalls. "It went through terrible throes. It ran into a storm headed to England, and it fell apart. It was really kind of disorganized."

On Wednesday, Aug. 19, things changed. Andrew started running into a strong high pressure area flowing down the Eastern Seaboard. Since a storm is a low-pressure system, it had to move away from

CHANGED EVERYTHING

NOTHING LEFT
Flora Carcina, 9, picks through the remains of the Everglades Labor Camp looking for her possessions. Some experts say farm worker families, impoverished to begin with, may suffer most in the long run: No insurance, no crops to work, no place to go.
C.W. GRIFFIN

the high pressure. It would either shift north, where it would quickly dissipate in the cooler waters of the North Atlantic, or it would be shoved west, where it would remain in the warm tropical waters that give storms their energy.

When the satellite maps showed Andrew heading west, Marks became excited. His specialty was measuring storms by airborne Doppler radar. In his 12 years as a hurricane researcher, he had

flown into hurricanes 300 times. Once, during Hugo, he was in a plane that lost an engine and almost crashed into the storm-tossed seas. In 1983, he rushed to Galveston, to record ground winds during Hurricane Alicia. There, he was in a building that experienced gusts of 92 mph; it was not a particularly scary experience.

The more Marks heard about Andrew, the more he liked it. The intense high-

pressure area served to ventilate the strengthening storm, stoking the flames of the hurricane's force.

At 5 a.m., Friday, Aug. 21, the hurricane center advisory announced: "Andrew begins to strengthen." That afternoon, Marks joined a team of scientists who flew to Puerto Rico to study the storm. Hurricanes are still mysterious, and scientists learn something new from every storm. "Our adrenaline was really pumping."

On Saturday morning, 800 miles east of Miami, with winds a little over 75 mph, Andrew became a hurricane. In his San Juan hotel room, Frank Marks stared at a map and, for the first time, he realized that the storm was headed directly at South Florida. Because of the high-pressure area, it would be virtually impossible for Andrew to change course. Still, as he prepared to fly into the storm, the image of Andrew hitting

WINDSWEPT

Shortly after dawn, the winds still not completely gone, these two women go to Dania Beach to see what happened. Their car became stuck in the sand, and they had to call a tow truck to pull them out.

MIKE STOCKER

his Miami home was only a vague abstraction.

PREPARATIONS BEGIN

From the air, Andrew was awesome, beautiful

In South Florida, veterans of previous hurricanes started getting ready. Judi Whiteman, a Dade resident for 40 years, knew supermarkets would be packed, and she was at hers before 7 a.m. Saturday. She loaded up with 30 gallons of drinking water, canned food, batteries and other items recommended for a hurricane.

Her husband, Richard, who works for Metro-Dade traffic management, began putting up their top-of-the-line storm shutters, which had cost them $8,200. As he worked, neighbors teased him that he was a worrywart, but the Whitemans wanted to make certain that they were ready for anything in their four-bedroom, $220,000 concrete block-and-stucco house in Country Walk.

From the air, Andrew seemed awesome and beautiful. Twice, the research plane carrying Frank Marks did figure eights through the storm. The flights, like most through hurricanes, were uneventful, and in late afternoon, the plane headed back to Miami.

As the day went on, hurri-

cane advisories became more ominous. At 11 a.m.: "Andrew continues to strengthen rapidly." At 2 p.m., with the storm 655 miles east of Miami: "The westward movement is expected to continue through Sunday, increasing the threat to South and Central Florida. Interests in that area should closely monitor advisories on this hurricane." At 5 p.m. Saturday, a hurricane watch was announced for Southern Florida, stretching up to Titusville.

In South Florida, people began flooding the supermarkets. At midnight, Herald reporter Tracie Cone found herself waiting for two hours in a line at an X-tra at Sample Road and State Road 7. Hundreds of people, some in pajamas and housecoats, were in the store, buying anything they could get. When Cone was still 20 carts away from the front of the line, the cashier suddenly announced she had worked 17 hours and was leaving. Cone and the others had to struggle to get into another line.

FROM THEORY TO REALITY
Scientist: 'This is going to be hell'

At 1 a.m. Sunday, Frank Marks returned to Miami and drove to his home in Sabal Chase. The research scientist had become the family man. Now Andrew was anything but academic. "This is going to be hell," he told his wife, Anita.

Early Sunday morning, as the announcement was made that the barrier islands would have to be evacuated, Marks began preparing his rental townhome in South Dade. He knew that, because hurricane winds churn counterclockwise, his greatest problem was going to be the eastern and northeastern bedroom windows. He boarded up all the windows he could and, in those places where he couldn't attach plywood to concrete, he taped them up. He moved all the valuables — stereo and television — to an upstairs closet, placed them up high, then pushed a dresser against the closet door.

Downstairs, Marks protected sliding glass doors with a bookcase, weighted down by a barbecue grill. He decided the safest place would be the family room, because its only window faced west. "This is where we stake our claim," he announced to his wife, 9-year-old daughter and a 10-year-old nephew who was staying with them. All the furniture was placed in the center of the room, along with mattresses. If necessary, Marks decided, their "escape hatch" would be a windowless half-bath off the family room. All emergency provisions — flashlights, batteries, a sleeping bag — went in there.

As he worked on the storm preparations, Marks received a call from a French hurricane expert who happened to be staying in a Brickell Avenue hotel. The hotel was closing, and the Frenchman didn't know where he and his wife should go. Marks invited them down. The Frenchman was excited: This was a rare chance for him to experience a hurricane.

PICKING UP THE PACE
Deciding to stay, deciding to go

All over South Florida, people were sweating under the hot sun, getting their places ready.

In Goulds, the Turcios family meticulously boarded up their shop, Things from Guatemala, one of a group of curio shops housed in quaint wooden structures behind the historic Cauley Square on U.S. 1. The Turcios knew their place was vulnerable, but they hoped for the best.

Near 88th Avenue and Coral Reef Drive, a little east of U.S. 1, Al Masso was putting up the aluminum shutters on the house he had lived in for 35 years. The shutters had been through three hurricanes. Many of the neighbors were evacuating, but the Massos had faith in their house and decided to stay put.

Not far away, Lowell Cooper knew he had to go. His $300,000 house was a half-mile east of Old Cutler, with only a thick tangle of bushes and trees between it and open water. An exposed spot, but Cooper, an insurance man, knew the concrete-block house had been designed to weather storms, with the living areas raised above ground level and windows protected by hurricane shutters. When the preparations were complete, Cooper and his family drove away in his Mercedes, headed to a rel-

BIG PICTURE

An Army Blackhawk flies over a badly damaged mobile home park near Harris Field in Homestead. The destruction was so widespread that only aerial views could give a feeling for the immense scope of Andrew's power.

DAVID WALTERS

ative's house in West Dade. Behind, in a ground-level garage, he left two perfectly restored cars: A 1928 Ford and a 1939 Ford V-8.

At 3:45 p.m., North Miami Beach High School, one of Metro's 48 shelters, was filled to capacity. At 4:15, water pressure dropped across the county as thousands filled their bathtubs. At 7 p.m., it was announced that Miami Beach was officially closed. Cars were allowed to leave, but none could enter. At 7:30, 20,000 were in shelters — less than a third of the 75,000 expected.

At 8 p.m., the National Hurricane Center announced the storm was 185 miles east of Miami. The hurricane was described as "extremely dangerous."

Hospitals were filling up. In South Dade, Baptist Hospital was barraged with calls. The elderly, people with heart conditions, diabetics — many wanted to be admitted. The staff said there was no room for those who didn't have a medical emergency, but, knowing that the extreme low pressure of a hurricane induces labor, they arranged for 225 women in their last trimester of pregnancy to camp out in the auditorium.

THE MOMENT OF TRUTH

'It's coming right across South Dade'

At midnight, a hundred journalists and meteorologists were packed into the National Hurricane Center, where usually only about 15 staffers work. Located on the sixth floor of a Coral Gables office building, the center's offices were the only ones that had hurricane shutters, but the staff was confident that the office could survive any problem.

Director Bob Sheets,

fueled by a constant supply of canned root beer, kept making live reports for the television stations. At 12:13 a.m. Monday, he announced: "Looks more and more like it's coming right across South Dade."

At 3 a.m., radar showed the center of the 140-mile-an-hour winds was 40 miles east of Miami. Hurricane-force winds stretched out 90 miles to the north from the center, and a somewhat shorter distance to the south.

At 4:28 a.m., the eyewall was entering southern Biscayne Bay. At 4:30 a.m., dispatchers ordered all police and fire personnel off the streets.

In the offices of the National Hurricane Center, reporters and staffers could feel the building sway. Everyone stopped for a moment, astounded at the eerie feeling of a sixth-story waving in the wind. One staff member announced he felt seasick.

A dazed reporter asked Sheets: "What direction is the building swaying?"

The ordinarily unflappable Sheets came as close as he ever did to losing his cool. "I don't know," he snapped. "You tell me."

Moments later, there was a large boom. Everyone froze. What was it? The radar suddenly went out. Apparently, the radar on the roof had tipped over. At 5:20 a.m., the wind gauge recorded a speed of 164 miles an hour. Then the gauge broke. From that moment on, whatever happened in Dade County was beyond measure.

BEGINNING TO PANIC
'This storm isn't like the other ones'

Off Coral Reef Drive, Al and Joyce Masso were beginning to panic. They could hear the metal shutters that had protected their house during 35 years of storms snapping in the wind. They retreated to the bedroom and slammed the door. They could hear glass breaking. The wind buckled the bedroom door. They slid a 200-pound dresser across the door. The screeching wind started moving the dresser. For the next two hours, they stood with their backs pressed against the dresser, pushing against the wind, wondering whether they were going to survive.

"This storm," mumbled Joyce, "isn't like the other ones."

In Sabal Chase, hurricane

FIRST LOOK
Heidi Hentshel, left, and Pilar Carrasco are overwhelmed by what they see at their South Dade trailer park.

PETER ANDREW BOSCH

13

expert Frank Marks gathered everyone in the family room. There were seven: four in the Marks family, the French couple and a neighbor. Marks had stayed awake throughout the night, fascinated by reports of the storm. The children slept for a while, but when the winds began screaming, everyone woke up. Suddenly, there was a loud pop. A window had blown. The house began shaking "like a bulldozer was pounding it."

He yelled for everyone to get in the bathroom. "I had drilled my kids, 'When I say go, don't ask questions. Just go.'" They went.

The tiny bathroom was large enough to house a toilet and sink. Into this cramped space squeezed five adults, two kids and Max, the cocker spaniel. No one was happy, particularly Max, who howled and whimpered as the wind blasted under the door.

Marks sat on the sink, the faucet rammed into his back, his feet braced against the door to keep the wind from blowing it in.

All his scientific detachment had vanished. He was awed — "I've never felt anything like it" — and afraid. His mind flooded with images of hurricane horror stories he had heard — ceilings splitting open, people sucked out by the wind. Now, there were no more precautions he could take, no scientific skill he could use to overcome the monster he had studied for so long.

"It was a little bit too close to home," he decided.

THE DOOR BUCKLES

Couple heads to closet, covered by a mattress

In their Country Walk house with the $8,200 shutters, Judi and Richard Whiteman hadn't been too worried. They had watched the news till 11:30, then slept to 4 a.m.,

when, as they expected, the loss of electricity woke them up. They stumbled out into the living room to see water dripping down. Without thinking, they went to get pails. Then they noticed that the front doors were buckling.

They threw themselves against the doors. Suddenly, the wind blasted the doors open. Richard was thrown against a wall. Judi was blown into a hallway. A four-foot-by-four-foot cupola floated through the door, spun in the air and then slammed to the floor. It was followed by a 15-foot board that flew through the air like a huge spear.

The expensive shutters were snapping. French doors blew out. The ceilings in the living area clunked to the floor. The Whitemans retreated to a bedroom. The ceiling there began to collapse. They went to the closet, crouching in six inches of water, with a mattress over them.

For a moment, the storm subsided. They could hear a small, battery-powered television that they had carried with them into the closet. Rick Sanchez of Channel 7 was saying that the eye was over South Dade. "The worst is yet to come."

Judi began crying. She was convinced she would never again see her son, away at a military academy in New Mexico. She couldn't imagine the house taking any more. Just then, they heard neighbors shouting. The house next door had collapsed and the six people inside needed a place to stay. The Whitemans invited them in, saying they were welcome to whatever protection their house could still provide.

Around 7 a.m., as the winds subsided, people began stumbling outside, to see what was left. Off Coral Reef Drive, the Massos found that the hurricane shutters that had survived 35 years of storms had simply disappeared. They weren't in the yard. They weren't anywhere. All the windows on the east side were blown out. Oddly, a Waterford crystal decanter that they had left on a table in the living area remained in place, unharmed, surrounded

by six crystal glasses, now filled with water.

In Sabal Chase, Frank Marks, the hurricane expert, found that only one window had broken. It was upstairs, on the northeastern side. All the family valuables, tucked away in closets protected by dressers, were "bone dry."

In Country Walk, the Whitemans found that Channel 7 had been wrong. The second part of the storm was a pussycat compared to the beginning, but their house was virtually totaled.

FACING THE LOSSES

Stomachs churn as owners check damage

Around 7:30 a.m., Lowell Cooper jumped in his Mercedes and drove to his home east of Old Cutler. He didn't take his wife, because he was afraid she couldn't stand the sight.

As he approached his house, his stomach began to churn. The streets were blocked by trees and debris. Cooper parked the Mercedes and walked the last few hundred feet, his fears growing with every step.

He had heard no discussion of storm surge on television, but that was because the wall of water had crashed ashore where there wasn't much development. Now, as Cooper reached his house, he saw what storm surge could do: His eastern garage wall — 20 feet long by eight feet high — was demolished.

Every concrete block had been blown out and scattered like toys. Leaves and seaweed littered what was left of the garage. The 1928 Ford had been lifted up, turned sideways and smashed into a wall. The 1939 Ford had crashed through the garage doors and spun around. Both cars were badly dented.

On the eastern side, most of his shutters were gone.

CRAMPED

Meteorologist Frank Marks, left, and family: He, six other people and Max, the cocker spaniel, ended up crammed into a half-bath.

WALTER MICHOT

Water had flowed through the raised living area, reaching a height of four feet, leaving a mark of seaweed and leaves on the walls. A kitchen counter had been swept away, the oven moved 12 feet.

The house had been filled with antiques — a grandfather's clock, an Oriental rug, a cherrywood chest that his great-great-grandmother had used. All were soaked and covered with debris.

Fighting back tears, Cooper mumbled, "Friends and family are the things that count now. We're alive. We've got our family."

And not much else. As a partner in a Perrine insurance business, he knew the storm would cost him. Homeowners insurance pays for wind damage, but federal insurance pays for flood damage, which was the bulk of his problem.

"The federal program doesn't recognize antiques," he said, finding a board from what had once been a beautiful stereo cabinet. "So if you lose a chair, they buy you . . . a chair."

AN UNTOUCHED PATCH
'Everything's OK. Miracles do happen'

In Goulds, Gustavo Turcios and his family went with great trepidation to see what had happened to their little shop, Things from Guatemala. All around it, the small wooden curio stores were ripped apart. But Turcios' had been under an almond tree, which had remarkably stayed intact. He looked inside, then emerged. Dazed, he mumbled, "It's a miracle. It's in one piece. Everything's OK. Miracles do happen."

At 8 a.m., Metro police director Fred Taylor warned that police would patrol South Dade and looters would be arrested.

DEVASTATED
On the island of Eleuthera, Christope Neely, 6, left, and his sister, Chrissonra, 8, rest by the remains of their home. Before hitting Florida, Andrew tore through the Bahamas, killing four.

CHARLES TRAINOR JR.

The warning didn't matter. By 11 a.m., at least 40 people had fanned through the Cutler Ridge Mall. They rushed through the demolished front of a Peaches music store and a Payless Shoe Store. As the looters were leaving, trucks filled with National Guardsmen drove up. One energetic soldier tackled a man who was running off with a pair of shoes and a bag of socks.

The storm cut a wide swath of destruction. Steel supports of billboards were twisted as if they were plastic. Splintered wooden structures looked from a distance like piles of toothpicks. Along the turnpike extension, one could see whole subdivisions that looked like developments under construction: Raw-wood roofs with no tar paper or shingles, windows with no glass. Trees everywhere were down. Shopping centers looked like the pictures of stores after the Los Angeles riots.

Everywhere, the storm had shown bitter impartiality, attacking the houses of rich and poor alike. Even the astute staffers of the National Hurricane Center were not immune. Three saw their houses virtually totaled.

Nothing looked like what it had been. Late Monday morning, Rod and Barbara Carlson realized what that meant when they drove back to their house east of U.S. 1 near Coral Reef Drive. They had lived there for 12 years, but as they weaved among the fallen power lines and downed trees, they didn't recognize anything. All street signs were down. Barbara felt a cold chill when she realized they had driven past their street without realizing it.

When they found their house, the roof was ripped off, the windows blasted. The motor for a ceiling fan was in their front yard — but it wasn't their ceiling fan.

GUARDING THE RUINS
'This is the worst. Ain't this the worst?'

At a strip shopping center in Naranja Lakes, Bud Nemeth sat numbly in front of Keg South, a beer-and-burgers place where he was the manager. A double-barrel shotgun rested on his lap. The tinted windows were unbroken, but the roof had collapsed. The inside was a wet mess.

"I spent the night here," Bud said numbly. His eyes were glazed, from exhaustion and shock. "I never want to do that again." He said he had turned 35 looters away that morning.

A few feet away, Jose Mar-

15

tino picked through wreckage of a business that had no roof, no window, no sign. Without thinking, a journalist asked, "What kind of business was this?"

Martino laughed hysterically. "Was," he repeated, glancing around, trying to absorb the fact his business was being mentioned in the past tense. "Spotlight Video," he responded at last, pointing at a soggy box of *The Addams Family movie*. "We rented video tapes."

Down the road, at the Coral Rock Mobile Home Park in Naranja Lakes, a young man with a scraggly beard, Scott Kuzusnik, stood amid mounds of debris, uncertain what to do. The trailer that he and Delora Reed had shared was now a pile of rubble. An orange-brown chair was on top of the pile, but it was the only recognizable item.

"There's a new bedroom set in there," he mumbled. "And a TV console."

"I lost my job," Reed said, "I couldn't pay our damn insurance. We've got nothing."

Kuzusnik was having a hard time believing that everything was gone. "This is the worst. Ain't this the worst?" he asked. Somehow, he figured, if this was the worst storm ever, it would make the suffering at least meaningful. To have lost all this for a second-rate storm...

Reed had more pressing concerns. "Where do we go for help? Is there going to be any help?"

THE PRESIDENT VISITS

Bush visits shelter, holds press conference

The journalist said he didn't know, but that President Bush was supposed to arrive in a couple of hours. "Well," Reed said, with a wry, slightly crazed smile, "perhaps he would like to come and have coffee here."

About 6 p.m., Air Force One touched down at Opa-locka Airport, emitting a motorcade of staff, Secret Service agents and the White House press corps. They roared south. When they spotted an uprooted tree at Miller Drive, the motorcade stopped and the president examined the tree. Then the group sped south, stopping briefly at a shelter, then racing to Cutler Ridge Mall, where Bush held a press conference in front of the Peaches that looters had ravaged.

With that, the motorcade roared back to the airport. The whole event, according to Herald photographer Al Diaz, lasted about two hours.

At 11 p.m. Monday, Flora Arzuaga, a Mexican migrant who built her own four-bedroom house with the aid of Centro Campesino, a self-help program for migrants, is standing in line hoping for food and water. "It took me 20 years to get my house," she says. "It took the wind an hour to destroy it."

The roof is gone. A gray, sandy lint coats everything: the beds, the dining room set, the sofas and chairs. Her family of nine sleeps with no roof, looking up at the stars. She uses rags for the baby's diapers. She worries about more rain, where they'll get water, their next meal. She worries about rats and disease. She worries the way she did before she left Mexico 16 years ago.

"Their spirits are still high," says Centro Campesino director Frank Navarro. "They'll snap back."

But Arzuaga looks at the floor and whispers: "I don't see how."

MIAMI BECOMES BEIRUT

As exhaustion sets in, tempers wear thin

By Tuesday morning, 24 hours after the storm had passed, exhaustion was setting in. Tempers were wearing thin. While Gov. Lawton Chiles was given a briefing at Metro's Emergency Management bunker, a gubernatorial staffer whispered to a Metro employee: "Do you have breakfast for the governor?" The Metro employee was aghast. Everyone in the bunker was hungry. Hurricane Andrew hadn't been exactly a catered affair.

"We have nothing but cookies and pickles," the Metro person replied.

On South Dade roadways, tourists were coming out in force, photographing and videotaping the wreckage. Traffic on the turnpike extension crawled along far worse than in any rush-hour traffic jam.

Fully armed soldiers were guarding stores and neighborhoods. Checkpoints were established on major thoroughfares, and people had to show I.D. Miami had become Beirut.

By Tuesday, good old American ingenuity was taking over. In Fort Lauderdale, a young man was spotted on busy Southwest 17th Street laboriously taping a long extension cord to the asphalt. He was running the cord from a neighbor's house on the side of the street with electricity to his side, which had none.

In South Dade, at the traffic circle where Sunset Drive meets Old Cutler, two budding capitalists, the Reece brothers, were selling 4,000-watt portable generators from a van. A cluster of Mercedes, Jaguars and a Buick were parked by the van as their owners checked out the merchandise.

"Fifteen hundred," said Michael Reece to a gray-haired man in a striped rugby shirt. "Sears is selling these for $3,500."

The man looked skeptical. He returned to his BMW and left.

"We're from Boca," Gregg Reece explained. "We drove up to Orlando and bought these at a Home Depot, then came down here. We tried Kendall, but the people there don't need generators, they need roofs."

In upscale neighborhoods near the traffic circle, the Reeces had done much better, selling 10 of the 12 they had bought. "Some people think we're doing a great job," Gregg said, "and others think we're gouging them." He managed a smug smile. "For once in our lives, we have something they want. You know, these guys are all lawyers and doctors in these neighborhoods, and you know what they charge. So we're here to pinch the people who've never been pinched, so they can have their ice cubes."

Gregg said they weren't making that much. The generators had cost them about $1,200 each, "so we're only making about $300." (Not exactly right: Home Depot in Orlando says it sold the 4,000-watt generators for $489, making the brothers' profit about $1,000 a unit.)

The Reeces broke off the conversation to talk to a young redheaded woman with a ponytail. She stared at the machine and learned it came with a day's supply of gas. "If it lasts one day," she told her companion, "I'll be happy." She pulled out her purse and wrote a check for $1,500.

The Reeces were accepting checks? "Well, sure," said Michael. "But most of these people are coming in nice cars, so we figure they're good for it, right?"

In the days following the storm, the long list of property casualties kept growing. Monkey Jungle had been virtually destroyed. The historic Deering Estate was torn up. The rainforest area of Fairchild Tropical Garden

DEFIANCE

Within a day, the people of South Dade announce that they aren't about to quit.

PATRICK FARRELL

was reduced to sticks. Metrozoo was badly damaged; officials announced it would be shut down for at least six months. The Metropolitan Correctional Center, which had housed former dictator Manuel Noriega and 1,400 other prisoners, was hit hard, and the prisoners were transferred.

Everywhere, people were crying for assistance, and there was little to give. Critics complained that the federal government seemed slow in organizing a relief effort. On Friday, Aug. 28, five days after the storm, The Herald's front

page blared in World War III-sized type: WE NEED HELP. Kate Hale, Dade's emergency director, came close to tears as she publicly begged for assistance: "Where the hell is the cavalry on this one? We need food, we need water, we need people."

The opening of public schools was postponed. So was the election. People tried frantically to cover their damaged roofs with plywood or plastic, but often the desperate repairs did little good: When a typical summer thunderstorm drenched South Dade, it set out a new wave of moans

as rain drenched still-soggy furniture.

On Sunday, Aug. 30, people stopped to give thanks for what they had left. In Florida City, a group of Mennonites held an open-air service on folding chairs outside their demolished church. By Monday, life was returning to normal for North Dade. Most people there had electricity, and authorities announced they no longer had to boil their water. In South Dade, however, the situation remained grim. Some residents began patrolling their ravaged neighborhoods, to

protect what little they had left from bands of roaming looters.

On Tuesday, Sept. 1, President Bush made his second trip in eight days to Dade County. The newly homeless saw him and begged: "Help us, Mr. Bush. Help Us." He promised to rebuild Homestead Air Force Base, but the next day some congressional leaders announced that they weren't certain it made financial sense to reconstruct the base.

Meanwhile, engineers and building inspectors were finding shoddy workmanship in

CAR SURGE

A day after the storm, traffic on U.S. 1 in South Dade backs up for miles as people try to get back to the Keys, which had been evacuated. The police set up roadblocks, permitting only Keys residents to get through.

CHUCK FADELY

many of the houses that had been wrecked by the storm. Older houses, it seemed, had held up much better than newer ones. In what was undoubtedly the beginning of a trend, several residents filed suits against the developers who had built their houses.

For those in the disaster area, the adventure of restoration was becoming a numbing grind. Some people were beginning to find shelter in the tent cities set up by the military, but accommodations were far from comfortable. The good-natured cooperation of the first few days was being tested as the tension and lack of sleep caught up with people. Complaints about domestic violence almost doubled — a problem exacerbated by the fact that the South Dade Safespace shelter for battered women had been destroyed in the storm.

Herald writer John Donnelly summed up the growing tension perfectly: "The truth is, this is getting old. The arguments, from everyone's open windows. The mess in the kitchen. The babies screaming in the heat."

Still, thousands of volunteers were trying to make things better. Police officers from as far away as Oklahoma were coming to help. Huge truckloads of food and supplies were streaming into South Dade, as well as the manpower to distribute them. Two weeks after the storm, 22,000 National Guardsmen and U.S. troops were in the area.

People were struggling to deal with what they had been through. For the first few nights after the storm, Judi Whiteman, the woman who survived the cupola flying into her living room, kept waking up at 4 a.m., the time she awakened when the storm hit.

"We've been married 29 years," Judi said. "We've saved and done everything right. Sometimes everything you do isn't enough. It's all gone in an instant. It's scary, you know. I'm still crying at times. I'll never be the same. But my husband and I are alive. We have faith in the Lord. I know during the storm we were praying constantly, not just for ourselves, but our friends and relatives, that everyone would get through it. And they did. But I didn't pray for this storm to go elsewhere. I couldn't wish this ill wind on anyone."

HERALD STAFFERS CONTRIBUTING TO THIS STORY:

Lizette Alvarez, Paul Anderson, Anne Bartlett, Don Bohning, Fran Brennan, Michael Browning, Jane Bussey, Tracie Cone, Al Diaz, John Donnelly, Elisabeth Donovan, Gail Epstein, Pamela Ferdinand, Tom Fiedler, Dexter Filkins, Don Finefrock, Sydney P. Freedberg, Bill Gato, Donna Gehrke, Lisa Getter, David Hancock, Dan Holly, Laurie Horn, Meg Laughlin, Donna Leinwand, Grace Lim, Phil Long, Arnold Markowitz, Patrick May, Gail Meadows, Martin Merzer, Gay Nemeti, John Pancake, Rhonda Prast, Karen Rafinski, Linda Robertson, Bill Rose, Lori Rozsa, Jim Savage, Tom Shroder, Peter Slevin, Luis Feldstein Soto, Charles Strouse, Rachel Swarns, Georgia Tasker, Don Van Natta, Jr., Bill Van Smith.

DIRECTIONS

On LeJeune Road, Al Darby, 65, usually a Metro train inspector, keeps traffic moving. With police handling emergencies, volunteers began directing traffic at busy intersections.

JEFFERY A. SALTER

DEFOLIATED

A sunset over the newly denuded Florida City: So many trees were felled or stripped bare that parts of the once-verdant South Florida landscape took on the look of a nuclear test site. Neighborhoods that had once been protected by shadows cast by dense clumps of trees were now exposed to glaring sunlight. As reporter Michael Browning observed: "There is simply too much sky."

CHARLES TRAINOR JR.

RICHARD, VICKIE BAROCAS

Richard Barocas, 37, spent the night with his wife, Vickie, 32, their dog, Spud, and a nephew, who thought the 30-year-old house in Mango Wood, 14700 SW 83 Ave., would be safe.

Richard lost his home, and he's not sure about his business. He owns a scuba diving store, and, he says, in this time of crisis, who would want to learn how to scuba dive?

Richard: "I didn't go to bed at all that night. My wife and my nephew went to sleep. I was tracking the storm via TV.

"When the power went, around 3, I woke them up. I said, 'It's starting. It's here.' It was only a few minutes after I woke them up, we were talking in the master bedroom, and we heard a loud noise. I peeked out our bedroom window and I saw trees bending, our screening from the patio had already ripped.

"While I'm watching, the whole screen pops out and flies. And I said, 'Let's go to the hall. Let's get out of here.'

"We closed the door to the hall; 10 to 15 minutes later our front window blew into

"'Ricky, are we going to die? Are we going to die?' And I kept saying, 'No, we are not going to die. We'll get out of this.'"

the house. We heard the glass. A few minutes after that, the opening into the attic in the hall came washing down and with that, water and insulation. The pressure in our ears was unbelievable.

"We got into a coat closet directly behind us. It was too small, so my wife and my nephew sat down. She was holding the dog. I was holding the door. Water started coming through the door.

"The sliding glass doors that lead to the pool blew out. You could hear them separating from the wall; they

were going Crrreeech. Then the water was real bad and the roof came down.

"You could hear it go. I was visualizing what was happening. You can hear the creeping of the nails as they get pulled. You could hear the noise getting closer. My wife kept asking me, 'Ricky, are we going to die? Are we going to die?' And I kept saying, 'No, we are not going to die. We'll get out of this.'

"We started discussing a plan. If the ceiling comes down, we have to hold on to each other and go to our cars. I told my wife she had to let go of the dog. She said she wouldn't. So I held the dog. But it never got to that point.

"The first peek I took, I opened the door and I saw the sky. So I shut it. I didn't want my wife to see it. 'Forget it,' I said. I didn't want to see it either."

– MIRTA OJITO

THE WINDS APPROACH

South Floridians scramble to ready for the rapidly moving storm

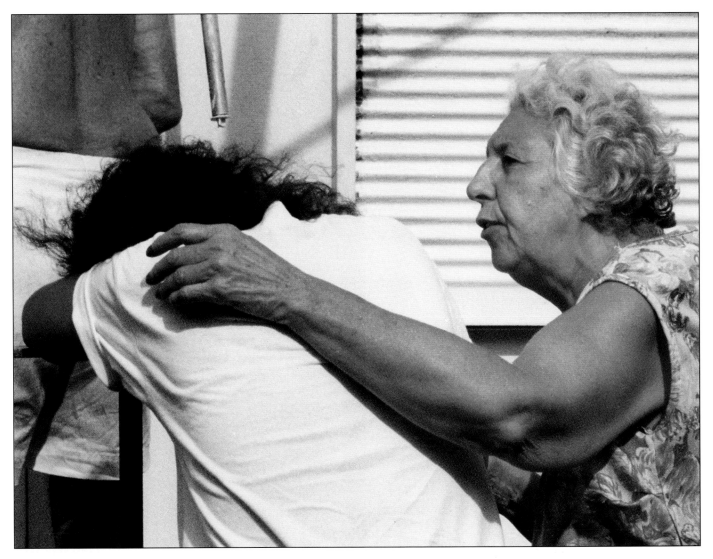

PLEADING

As the storm approaches, Violet McGlen tries to reassure her daughter, Cora Dickey, left, that she will be OK. Cora had come from her West Broward home to beg that her mother, staying in Hollywood, evacuate the area. Violet at first didn't want to leave, but finally relented.

A. ENRIQUE VALENTIN

ANSWERED PRAYER

The owners of Neon Signs on Davie Boulevard in Fort Lauderdale leave an urgent request on their plywood. Broward ended up suffering little damage.

BETH A. KEISER

FINAL PREPARATIONS

Before leaving Hollywood with her daughter, Violet McGlen makes certain the house is well protected. Because of somber advance warnings from the National Hurricane Center, most South Florida residents prepared carefully for the storm.

A. ENRIQUE VALENTIN

RUSH HOUR

Throughout South Florida, people flock to supermarkets for last-minute supplies before Andrew arrives. The stores were so packed that sometimes customers had to wait two hours to get to the cashier.

BILL FRAKES

"Sunday we were trying to evacuate people. Nobody was thinking about disaster recovery."

THOMAS HERNDON, GOVERNOR CHILES' CHIEF OF STAFF

EVACUATED

Residents of the Gem Care Center on South Beach prepare for a bus ride to their shelter, a nightclub in Opa-locka. Though most of the center's 200 residents are in their 80s and 90s, their transfer went smoothly. Altogether, about 700,000 people in South Florida were asked to abandon their residences.

JON KRAL

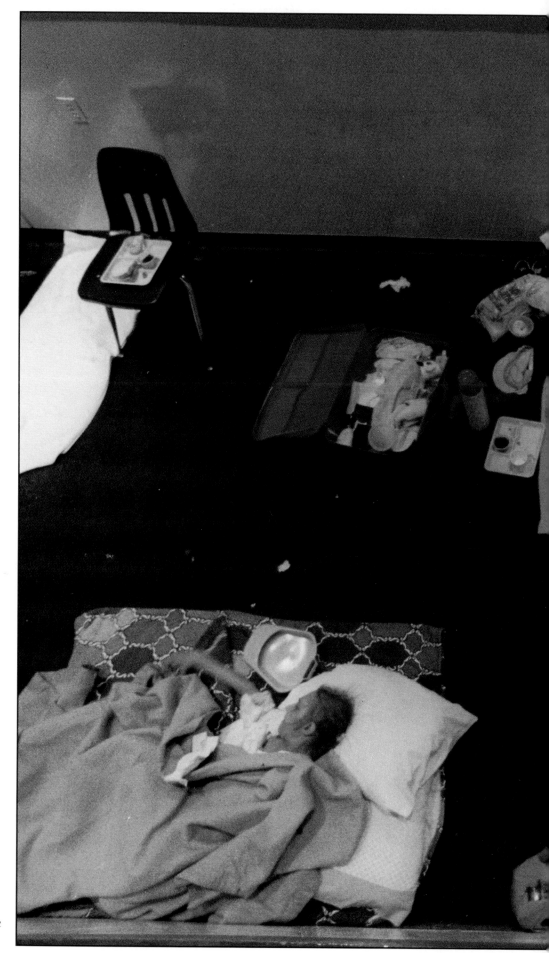

GIMME SHELTER

Elderly residents pack Hallandale High School. A special ward was set up for the sick. About 80,000 ended up in shelters. Many other evacuees stayed with friends.

MIKE STOCKER

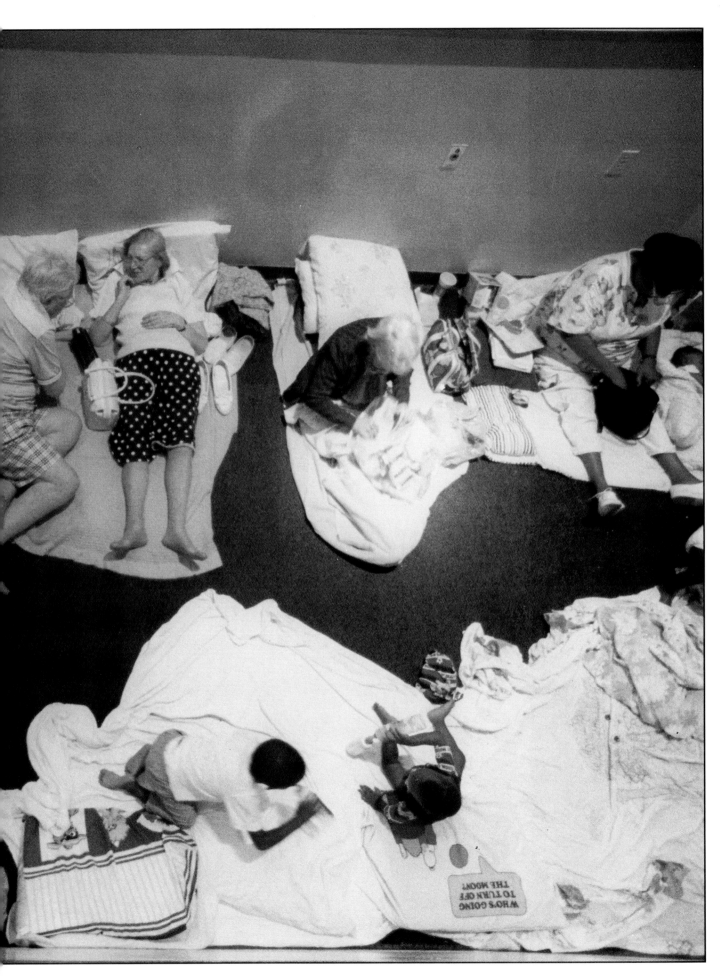

"Coral Gables south heavily damaged, railroad track torn up. Shopping centers leveled in Homestead area."

THE FIRST REPORT AFTER THE STORM, FROM STATE POLICE AT 7:50 A.M.

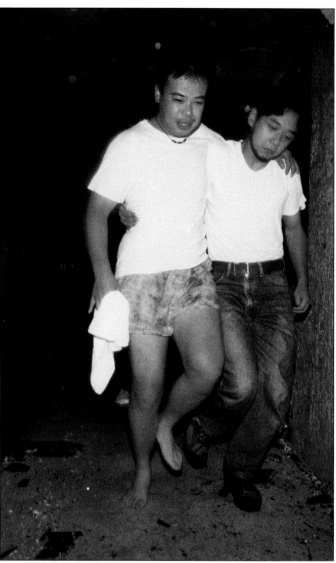

NO ROOM

While Andrew's eye passes overhead, one Japanese tourist helps another whose foot was cut by glass. They were struggling down a corridor at the Comfort Inn in Florida City, seeking a safer room after their own was demolished.

C.M. GUERRERO

POLICE HELP

A grandmother hugs her granddaughter. Even before the driving rain stopped, people whose homes had been devastated sought refuge in the Florida City police station.

C.M. GUERRERO

ALDO GUERRERO

Guerrero, 36, was in a hotel in Orlando with his family when he heard about the hurricane. A kid in the hotel pool had teased his son Andrew, 8, about having the same name as the hurricane that was about to hit South Florida.

Alarmed, Aldo got in the car with his family — wife Joanne, 34; son Daniel, 7; and son Andrew, and headed south, to their home near Homestead Air Force Base.

But then they heard about evacuation plans for the neighborhood, so they went to West Kendall to spend the night with Joanne's brother, who is a member of the SWAT team. Guerrero, who later learned he had lost his own home, figured they would be safer in Kendall. He figured wrong.

Aldo: "I helped my brother-in-law board up his house. There were eight of us in the house. My family and my brother-in-law, Danny Formosa; his wife, Pam; their baby, Danielle [8 months old] and my wife's mother, Ann.

"The wind woke me up at about 2:30. My brother-in-law was waking everybody up.

"We were holding on for dear life."

"We went into the family room. The wind was getting so strong that me and my brother-in-law were holding the front door with all our strength. But it got to the point when we couldn't hold anymore. We counted to three and let go of the door, each running in a different direction.

"We screamed for everybody to get into the bathroom in the hall. As soon as we let go of the door, it popped open. The wind came in and it took the walls around the sliding door in the back. The ceiling and the roof were coming down around us. The kids were screaming.

"Our ears were popping from the pressure as we ran to the bathroom. We got into the bathroom, and my brother-in-law and I were again holding the door. We were looking at each other like, 'This is it. It looks as if we don't hold this door, we

are flying out of here.' We were holding on for dear life. We could hear everything in the house going, 'Pa-Boom!' Everything was falling down. It sounded like a Fourth of July celebration.

"Water was seeping in through the air vent. We were collecting buckets of water and dumping them in the sink, but the water was coming back through the bathtub. We put pillows all the way to the ceiling to protect the baby and the kids. It was a small space. We were real tight in there; we couldn't breathe.

"It was a scary moment. The only thing that kept me going was the radio. It was like a connection to the world. We were holding that door with our backs for about three hours. We got bruises all over. Everybody was white as a ghost in there, and quiet. Everybody was praying. That's why we were so quiet, I think."

— MIRTA OJITO

DAWN OF DESTRUCTION

After the awful howl, we awoke to see South Florida with a changed face

CURIOS
Hazel Mueller makes her way through the debris of the shops at historic Cauley Square near Goulds. Most of the curio and antique shops were badly damaged.

CHUCK FADELY

STUNNED
Heidi Hentshel despairs at
the destruction of her home
at the Dadeland Mobile
Home Park.
PETER ANDREW BOSCH

CRUMPLED

Airplanes look like they had been dropped on the runway. About 90 percent of the airplanes at Tamiami Airport
were reported to have been destroyed. The tower was severely damaged, and looters roamed through the wreckage,
stealing electronic gear and whatever else they could.

JOE RIMKUS JR.

DESPAIR
In Little Havana, a person stumbles through the early morning rain as Andrew departs. Most areas of the city of Miami, North Dade and Broward suffered only minor damage, with downed trees causing the greatest problems.

JEFFERY A. SALTER

CYCLE TIME

About 8 a.m., people on Sunset Drive near South Miami emerge to see what Andrew had wrought.

PETER ANDREW BOSCH

OBSTACLES

Cars weave around a downed traffic signal at Southwest 107th Avenue. The hurricane knocked out about 1,900 of Dade's 2,300 traffic lights. The county's drivers responded by being uncommonly courteous — for the first few days.

PATRICK FARRELL

LEFT TURN
YIELD
ON GREEN

STOPPED

On Highway 836
west of the airport, a
huge overhead sign
crashed down,
crushing this taxi.
C.W. GRIFFIN

RAVAGED

From the air, Country Walk looks like it had been hit by a nuclear weapon. Perhaps 90 percent of the community's 1,700 homes were destroyed, and some residents filed suit against the developer, charging that shoddy construction was to blame.

BILL FRAKES

ANGUISH

Jeanette Peralta is devastated by the damage to her house in Coral Reef Gardens. This side of her house appeared intact, but other windows had been blasted out, and the inside was almost gutted.

PATRICK FARRELL

FREED

A monkey frolics on a dead power line. More than 2,000 research monkeys escaped after the storm. Because people wrongly believed that some of the primates carried the AIDS virus, more than 200 were killed by fearful residents.

PETER ANDREW BOSCH

BEST FRIENDS

Andy Valdes carries his two dogs across the bridge to his Fort Lauderdale beach home. Valdes, forced to evacuate, made the mistake of spending the hurricane with friends in Kendall.

BETH A. KEISER

44

RESCUED

Diane Clark and daughter Sheena were able to rescue their cat but not much else from their demolished trailer at the Dadeland Mobile Home Park. Since pets weren't permitted in shelters, people had to leave them behind. Many cats and dogs were able to find hiding places and survived.

PETER ANDREW BOSCH

TIPPED

Mark Futch sits listening to his radio on Southwest 6th Avenue in Homestead. The town of 25,000 saw 80 percent of its homes destroyed. What had once been a quiet farm-oriented community on the edges of an urban megalopolis had become a scene of unrelenting ruin.

CHARLES TRAINOR JR.

PRECEDING PAGE
MAROONED

A sailboat lies two blocks inland in what used to be a wooded area of South Dade. The dangerous storm surge didn't do as much damage as experts feared, partly because the waves hit the coast in an area that wasn't heavily developed.

PATRICK FARRELL

STUNNED DISBELIEF

Minutes after Andrew passed, Margarita Llano still can't believe that the winds could be so powerful that they ripped a wall off her South Dade house. She was clutching her son Enrique, 4, and a relative, Elizabeth Castro, also 4. More than a dozen people had sought refuge with her before the storm, imagining her house near Country Walk was in a safe location.

PETER ANDREW BOSCH

AFTERMATH

Jose Navado, holding his son Cristian Santos, bursts out crying as he surveys the ruin of his mobile home. Trailer parks were so badly damaged by the storm — their debris flying sometimes for blocks — that some experts suggested they be prohibited in South Florida.

PATRICK FARRELL

EXPOSED

Residents return to the Saga Bay Apartment complex, at 212th Street and Biscayne Bay, to find soggy furniture and no windows. A resident lowers his belongings to the street below. The American Red Cross estimates that 9,140 apartments were destroyed, along with 8,140 homes and 8,230 mobile homes.

CHUCK FADELY

BLASTED

A damaged F-16 sits at the devastated Homestead Air Force Base. President Bush requested $480 million to rebuild the base, but Congress was hesitant.

CHUCK FADELY

DESOLATION ROW

Kenneth Dykes looks around the place where he used to live: The Dadeland Mobile Home Park. The trailer that his father had reconstructed was no longer habitable. The park, located near Country Walk, was one of the places hardest hit by the storm.

BILL FRAKES

LOST

Amid the wreckage of the Coral Rock Mobile Home Park in Naranja, this old souvenir photograph lies in the rubble. Many people lost all their family mementos in the storm.

CHUCK FADELY

DRIVING BY

Many cars had windows blasted out by the storm, and South Dade's highways took on the appearance of a demolition derby.

AL DIAZ

AGROUND

This boat and its three crewmen started the storm two miles offshore. The boat ended up in the yard of this estate.

CHARLES TRAINOR JR.

LEVELED

In Homestead, exotic Australian pines look like they had been mowed down. So many trees were
damaged that one expert said it would take nurseries a decade to replace the lost foliage.

JOE RIMKUS, JR.

NO MORE TV

The historic Deering Estate, facing the bay off Old Cutler, was hard hit, and the stand of royal palms, which often appeared on *Miami Vice*, was flattened.

CHUCK FADELY

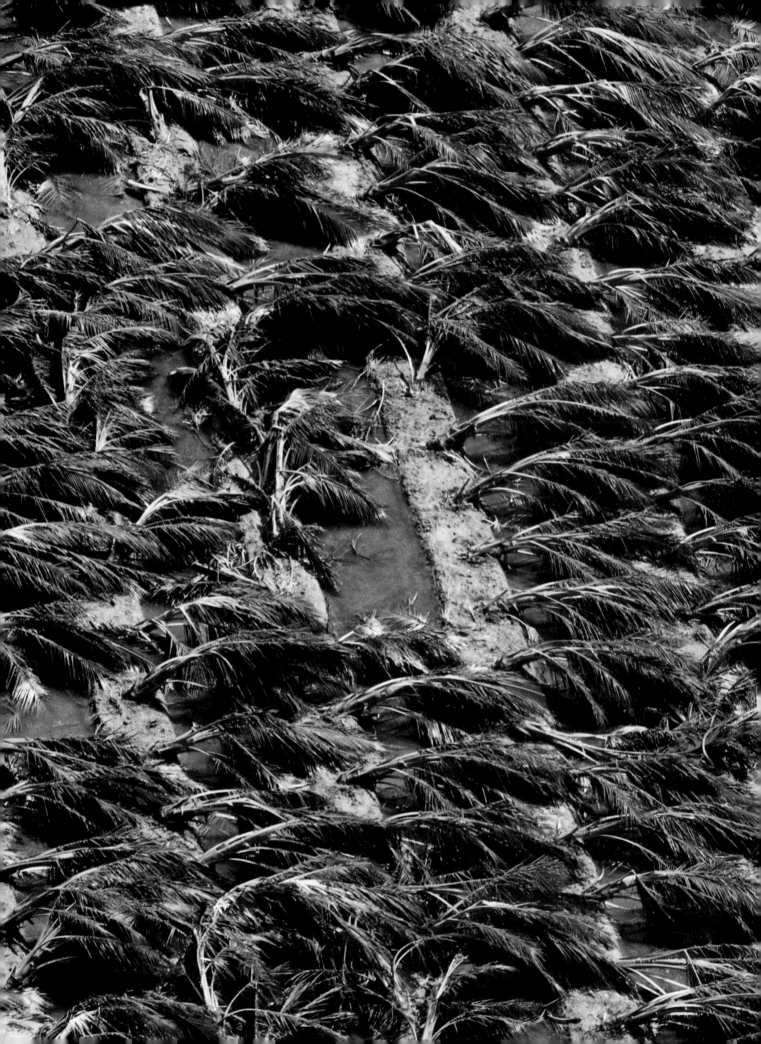

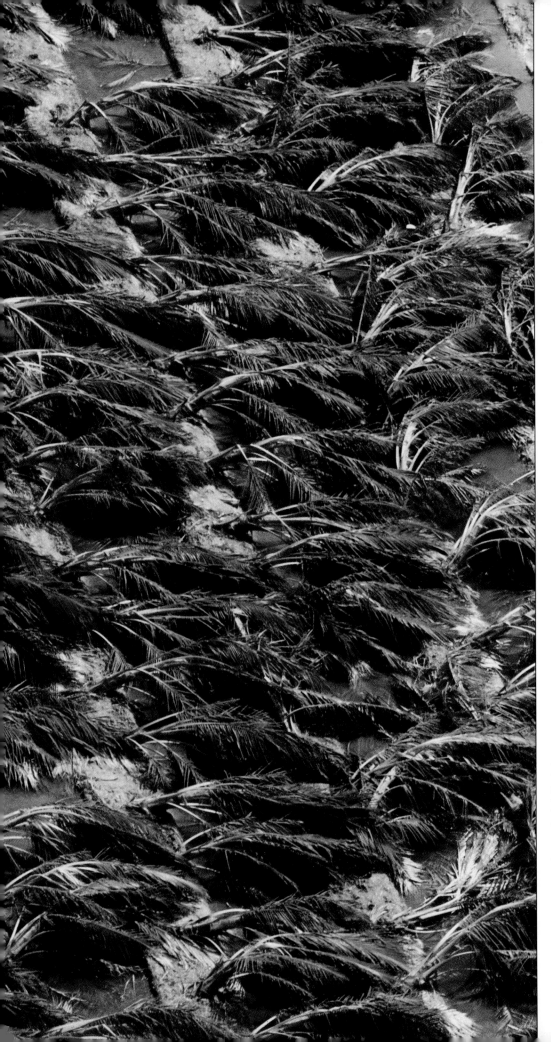

FIELD OF WOE

No palms are left
standing in this
Homestead nursery.
Officials estimate that
10,000 acres of nurseries
were ruined. Altogether,
about 80 percent of
Dade's 3,655 farms were
damaged. Total loss to
the county's agriculture:
$1.04 billion.

CHUCK FADELY

63

PACKING UP
Scott Percell retrieves a few belongings from his house in the Courtyards at Deerwood.

C.W. GRIFFIN

DIGGING OUT

Lou Rae LaPointe carries possessions through the tunnel that she had to dig to get out of her house buried in trees.

PATRICK FARRELL

PRAYER

Doyle Green, 74, who has lived on a houseboat near the Card Sound Bridge for three decades, gives his personal assessment of what the storm meant. Many other people were thinking: "There but for the grace of God go I."

RICK McCAWLEY

IMPALED

At the Matheson Hammock marina, Warren Lindau inspects his 42-foot sailboat, Wasuli. The bow was submerged, the stern impaled on a piling.

CHUCK FADELY

WIPE OUT

At the Dinner Key Marina, 124 boats sank or were destroyed and 175 were badly damaged. The losses forced the cancellation of the Columbus Day Regatta, the premier event for yachtsmen.

PATRICK FARRELL

SKYLIGHT

Sharon Hench looks up at the huge holes in the roof of her Country Walk home. During the storm, she and her husband, Michael, dashed from room to room to survive.

BILL FRAKES

SHORE WATCH

From inside a gutted Old Cutler mansion, a security guard watches over a beached freighter. The captain hired the guard after looters tried to steal equipment from the ship.

MICHELLE PATTERSON

NOTHING LEFT

In the South Miami Heights section near the Florida Turnpike, people search for their belongings in a house ripped apart by the storm.

C.W. GRIFFIN

NEW LOOK
An explorer picks his way through what appears to be a dense field. It was actually the entrance to the upscale development of Cocoplum off Old Cutler Road.

BILL FRAKES

FINAL PLEA
Wind whips through the shattered window of a battered wood-frame house in Florida City. The praying hands were left behind by the departed residents.

CANDACE BARBOT

NO HORSING AROUND

Betty Fagan took her pet horse of 21 years, Buttercup, into the house with her for protection, but after the roof and doors blew out, Buttercup bolted outside, where she was trapped between the house and a fallen tree. "Wouldn't you put your horse in your house when a storm was coming?" Betty asked afterward. "I had no other place to put him."

C.W. GRIFFIN

A NEW ART FORM

So many helicopters — filled with government officials, supply teams and news photographers — were whirling around South Dade that some residents developed a new creative medium: roof art. Some people were able to keep their sense of humor — at least for a while.

CHUCK FADELY

77

STEVE, FERN GOODMAN

Steve Goodman took his parents, an aunt and a cousin to his house near The Falls. His parents live by the bay in Miami. His aunt and cousin live in Surfside. They thought they would be safer inland, way south. But Steve and his family almost lost their home and their lives.

He's not complaining, though. Steve, 37, and his wife, Fern, 35, are taking Andrew with a positive attitude and a lot of laughs. They are lucky, they said. They have a Sir Speedy printing business on Biscayne Boulevard. They are young. They can rebuild. And, most importantly, the kids — Erin, 4, and Jeffrey, 8 — are fine.

Steve: "I woke up at about 2:15, looked out my bedroom window, saw some trees starting to move. Thought it was time to get ready, got up, got dressed. I woke the wife up, asked her to get dressed. I went to bed at 10 o'clock because I knew I'd get up early. Made enough noise in the house to wake up the family.

"I had decided that my daughter's bedroom, in case there was a problem, that we

> *"It was just the most unbelievable thing. We had a few conversations with The Man upstairs."*

would hide in there. We were in the living room, listening to the radio, just talking about the storm. Something hit the back of the house, and it scared us all and we ran to the bedroom. I didn't even have to say, 'Go!'

"I grabbed a mattress from the bed and threw it on the door and shortly thereafter windows started going in the house. You heard glass going, the wind shattering the glass. We were listening to the radio. I'm holding the mattress and holding the door shut with my father and my wife. My mother, my aunt, the kids were in the closet, my cousin was under the desk. The puppy dog, Jacque, was in the garage.

"I thought it was going to

come to an end. The house shook, the pressure in my ears. Water was seeping in. It was like being in an airplane. You heard the wind blowing, you heard windows breaking. Water was seeping in. A couple of times I thought I wasn't going to make it. It was just the most unbelievable thing. We had a few conversations with The Man upstairs."

"As the wind died down, I would get a little gutsy, grab a flashlight and venture a little out. At that point, ceilings were falling. The roof tiles were being blown off, water was seeping through the plywood. The ceilings were drenched. My fence was gone. Windows were gone. The water destroyed the inside of our house. The furniture is ruined. But there was no damage to the room where we were. Somebody looked out for us."

— MIRTA OJITO

WE NEED HELP

One hundred hours of disorder and delay impede relief for the hurricane victims

MOVING OUT

A family of Mexican migrants loads newly received supplies into their badly damaged car. Their house had been destroyed, and they were staying with friends. The day after this photo was taken, the family moved to Tennessee.

JEFFERY A. SALTER

"Where the hell is the cavalry on this one? We need food, we need water, we need people."

KATE HALE

FRAZZLED

Kate Hale, director of Dade's emergency management office, struggles to cope with a myriad of crises that confronted her. Coordinating local, state and federal relief efforts did not go smoothly at first.

PATRICK FARRELL

COMMAND CENTRAL

Leaders of Metro, police, fire, utilities, schools and other groups operate out of a West Dade bunker that was originally designed for nuclear wars.

RICK MCCAWLEY

SEARCHING

Ed Rigolo, a Palm Beach County search and rescue officer, and his dog Mara hunt for bodies in the rubble of a migrant trailer park in Florida City.

PATRICK FARRELL

GASSING UP

Near Red Road and U.S. 1, cars line up for gas after the storm. Even for those whose property didn't suffer major damage, Hurricane Andrew had a way of making life miserable for a few days.
PATRICK FARRELL

MAKING DO

Javier Erazo uses a battered but functioning pay phone to call relatives in Honduras and Guatemala. For several days, so many Dade residents were using the phones that Southern Bell officials begged people to limit their calls.

AL DIAZ

NEXT PAGE

SMALL COMFORT

A 13-year-old girl named Maria recovers a doll from the wreckage of her home at the Quail Roost Mobile Home Community.

JON KRAL

PHONE HOME

Lines form for the only working phone for a mile in central Homestead. Many wanted to call relatives to assure them they were OK. Considering the strength of the storm, casualties were remarkably light. In the state, authorities reported that only 15 deaths could be attributed directly to the storm and another 23 indirectly. Counting the dead in the Bahamas and Louisiana, Andrew killed 51 people — a fraction of the 6,000 that died during the 1900 Texas hurricane.

ALAN FREUND

GIVING AID
William Foy, 90, lies on the parking space in front of where his mobile home used to be. He was preparing bandages to dress the wounds his wife had suffered.

C.M. GUERRERO

WATER LINE
People in South Dade even have to wait in line for a jug of water after officials warned that tap water might be contaminated.

CHUCK FADELY

FAST SERVICE

People carry food and drinks out of a badly damaged Circle K convenience store near SW 268th Street and 128th Avenue. Some took only supplies they needed. Others grabbed what they felt like.

C.W. GRIFFIN

FLEEING

A looter tries to hide his face with shoes he just pulled out from a store on Southwest 152nd Street. Looting was rampant throughout South Dade, beginning soon after the storm left.

AL DIAZ

ON GUARD

Members of the Florida National Guard patrol a strip shopping center on U.S. 1. Guardsmen could watch over property, but weren't empowered to make arrests.

AL DIAZ

Not since the advent of the refrigerator have so many people looked so desperately for such a simple commodity as ice.

CHILLED

Residents come away from a relief station with cool comfort. Without electricity for refrigerators or air conditioning, ice became uncommonly valuable.

WALTER MICHOT

ICEMEN COMETH

Local volunteers shovel ice from a truck that came from Bradenton. After hearing that ice was selling for up to $5 a bag in the devastated areas, some good Samaritans in the Gulf Coast city filled the truck with ice and drove it to South Dade, where they distributed it free.

C.W. GRIFFIN

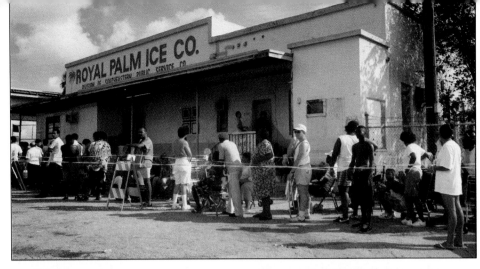

WAITING

Desperate for anything to keep food cool, people line up for blocks to get ice on South Dixie Highway. It could take two hours to reach the front of the line.

MARICE COHN BAND

FIGHTING BACK

Loretta Landrum, holding a .357 Magnum with hollow point bullets, takes turns with her husband guarding their Perrine home while they wait for the insurance adjuster to arrive.

MARICE COHN BAND

DEAD OR ALIVE

As this warning on a Homestead hotel shows, South Dade took on a bit of the flavor of the Wild West for the first few days. Both good guys and bad guys were armed, and sometimes it wasn't easy to tell who was who.

CARL JUSTE

FULLY ARMED

An exhausted Ron Williams keeps watch over his house in the Villages of Homestead. He had already chased off one looter, and he wanted to make certain he was ready for anything.

PATRICK FARRELL

FAMISHED

Juan Busto and many others wait for food at Loren Roberts Park in Homestead. After hours of standing in line, the first food supply ran out. Disappointed and hungry people were starting to leave when a tractor-trailer truck arrived loaded with food gathered by the Florida Jaycees. Guardsmen had to restrain the crowd.

AL DIAZ

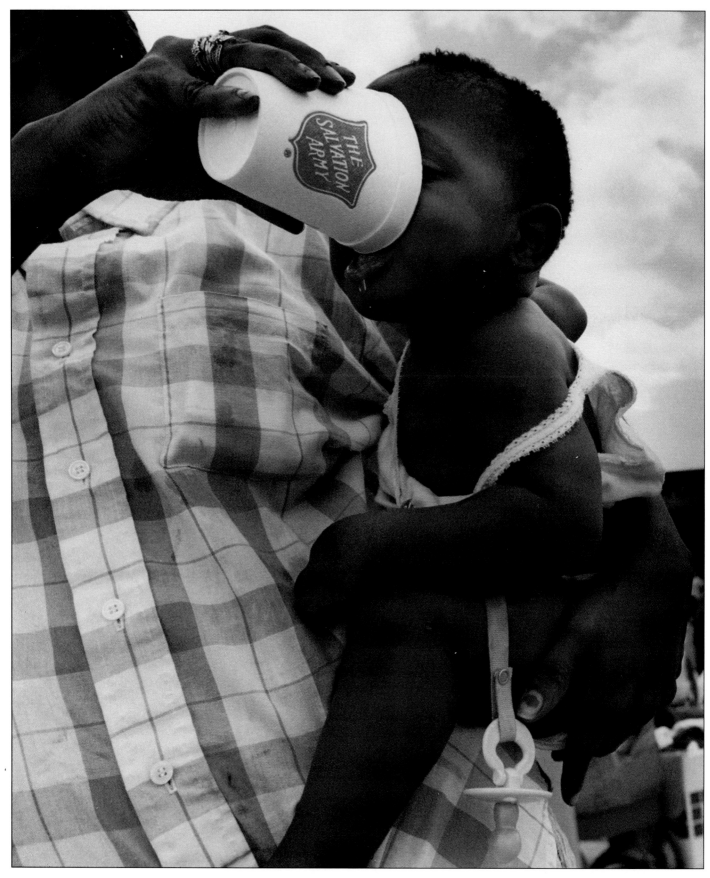

QUENCHING

Napolean Howard Jr., 5 months old, gets a cool drink of water at an aid site manned by the Salvation Army in a supermarket parking lot.

JEFFERY A. SALTER

Cleansing

Kerline Maydal washes her son Jonathan Maydal in a Homestead yard. Authorities were worried that contaminated water might lead to illnesses of epidemic proportions.

Jeffery A. Salter

Sending a Message

Many people stop by to ask this fellow about Grandma Newton, who ran a well known bed-and-breakfast place across the street. When people saw her place was demolished, they went across the street to ask about her. Finally, the fellow decided it would be simpler to erect this sign.

CHARLES
TRAINOR JR.

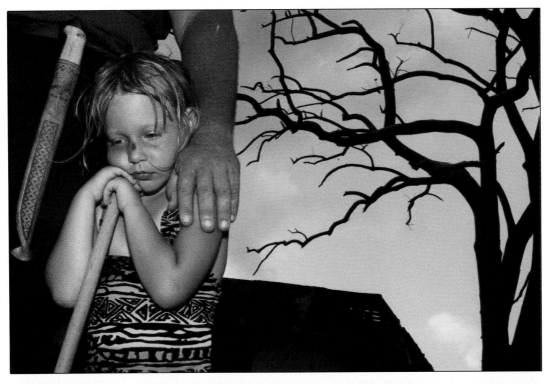

EXHAUSTION

Sometimes, all the effort gets to be too much: Genesah Duffy, 4, is comforted by her father, Jack. Their family was sleeping in a tent outside their house. A few days after the storm, local psychiatrists attended a seminar to discuss Andrew's long-term effects on children.

PATRICK FARRELL

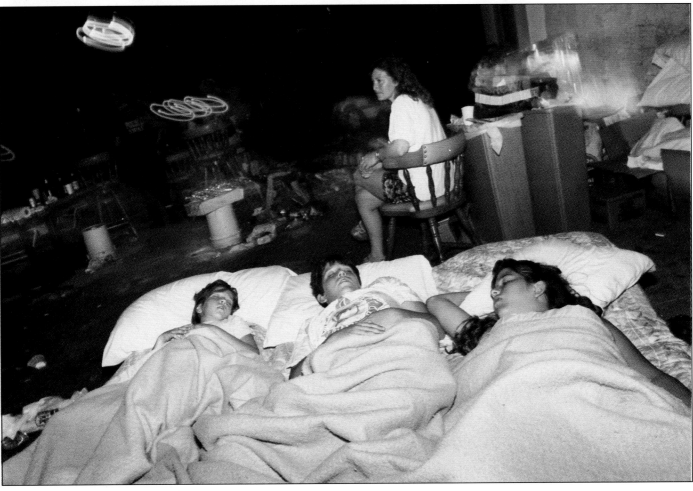

UNCERTAIN REST

Outside a devastated Days Inn that their father owns, three children fall asleep in the parking lot. From left: Katrina Hatem, 10; Andrew, 12; and Angela, 14. Their mother, Ellen, watches over them from a chair.

PATRICK FARRELL

VICTOR, PAMELA SABDUL

"It's something you can't talk about. You just have to see it."

Victor Sabdul, 41, knew he was supposed to evacuate his two-story home in Cutler Landings near Homestead Air Force Base, but he decided to stay. After all, the house was only about 4 years old and he had been through hurricanes before in Jamaica. He boarded up some windows and prepared to spend the night with wife Pamela, 40, and children Kimal,16, and Jilian,10.

The family survived, but the house did not. Thursday morning there wasn't a dry spot in the house. Plastic flowers were scattered on the wet carpet. Father and son were boiling an egg for lunch in the garage. A wet white slipper with a pink flower was lying on top of a heap of glass on the second floor.

Victor: "I never went to sleep that night. We were watching TV in the living room when the hurricane started brewing. It was about three o'clock when the lights went out.

"Then a window went behind us and things started flying. My son and I ran with a piece of plywood to put on the window. But then, every window started going: Plum! Plum! Glass was exploding all over. And then, Plum! went the front door. We found it on the floor 15 feet away. And then Plum! the back door went. The hurricane was here. And it had the house all to itself.

"We said, 'Let's go. To heck with this!' And we ran downstairs. We hid in this little room. We thought that room was going to explode too. The shingles on the roof were going, Pop! Pop! Pop! Have you ever heard the sound of shingles going? My wife and my daughter were screaming, crying. It was one of those situations where you don't know if you are going to be alive or not the next morning. My son and I were leaning against the door. It was like a nightmare.

"Then, when the eye passed over and it was calm, we heard somebody banging at the door. It was the neighbors, two teenage girls and their mother. They were screaming, 'Please let us in. We lost our roof!' We couldn't find the key to the door. So we opened the garage. They came to the room with us and then the wind started again.

"It was bad. Very bad. When we came out of there, I was glad we were alive and in one piece. It's something you can't talk about. You just have to see it."

– MIRTA OJITO

HOPE AMID CHAOS

Revved-up effort kicks in at last

STANDING FAST
Guardsman Scott Merrick, 25, stands watch in darkened South Dade. As the number of troops expanded to more than 20,000, South Dade took on the appearance of an armed camp.

PATRICK FARRELL

101

VOLUNTEERS

Paul Barrow dresses like a soldier, but he's a volunteer, distributing food in South Dade. Many people were desperate for food but couldn't get to the relief sites, and Barrow joined with several friends to get the food to the people.

Before the military arrived, some citizens took relief efforts into their own hands.

AT THE READY
Roger Worley watches as Barrow and other volunteers deliver supplies. Because crowds mobbed their truck, they developed the habit of moving in quickly, dropping the food and leaving before a crowd surrounded them.

MARICE COHN BAND

SUPPLIES
David Jones, 4, starts off looking for a can of fruit cocktail among the boxes of supplies brought by Barrow. He didn't find it, but got plenty of other food.

MARICE COHN BAND

WATER, WATER

At a South Dade emergency center, hundreds of bottles
of water were lined up.

BILL FRAKES

PILED HIGH

A woman examines contributions. Mounds of supplies were donated by concerned people throughout the United States. After several days, officials said they had far too much clothing and asked people to stop sending it.

RICK MCCAWLEY

HOT WORK

Taquinnia Lee wipes sweat away as she and her friend Jackie Mills pull a wagon loaded with supplies from a relief site at Florida City Park. The heat was often stifling as people endured the long lines for food.

PETER ANDREW BOSCH

BEATING THE HEAT

A volunteer cools off with a shower at the Everglades Labor Camp. Relief work under the brutal summer sun was exhausting.

AL DIAZ

WAITING

Postal guards watch over the crowds waiting to receive their mail.

JOE RIMKUS JR.

MAIL CALL

A line stretches for blocks of people waiting for mail at the Quail Heights Branch Post Office. In a disaster zone, even the smallest task becomes an immense chore.

CHUCK FADELY

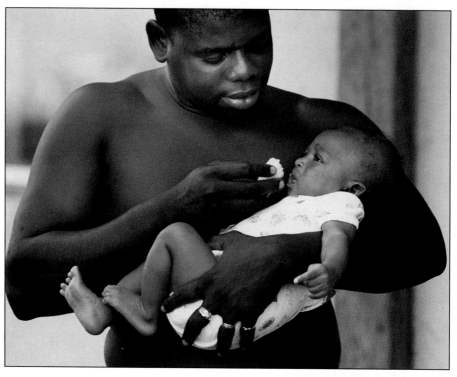

HELPING OUT

At the Caribbean West Apartments, Anthony Arda feeds Adaruis, 3 months.

CHARLES TRAINOR JR.

SUSTENANCE

A somber Cleman Pierre receives food at Loren Roberts Park in Florida City on Wednesday, two days after the storm hit. The relief effort was still not well organized and it caused delays.

AL DIAZ

FROM BROWARD, WITH LOVE

In Homestead, residents wait grimly for Dade County employees to hand out food donated by Coral Springs residents. Private donations were getting to people more quickly than government relief.

CANDACE BARBOT

CONVOY

A day after President George Bush orders them into action, a convoy of U.S. Army vehicles moves down 312th Street in Homestead, delivering portable kitchens. By day's end, five were operating. Others were on the way.

PATRICK FARRELL

"This is catastrophic beyond comprehension."

LYNNE KEATING
FEMA SPOKESPERSON

POWERLESS

Florida Power & Light crews work around the clock, but there were so many downed lines that it took weeks to get power restored in some areas.

WALTER MICHOT

ON PATROL

A week after the storm, two members of the 82nd Airborne, Pfc. Bret Fisher, left, and Lt. Kevin Quarles patrol a mobile home park in Homestead.

BILL FRAKES

TUGGING

Soldiers of the 82nd Airborne help remove a felled tree from the yard of a Cutler Ridge home.

JEFFERY A. SALTER

MODERN CAVALRY
Soldiers of the 82nd Airborne Division from Fort Bragg, N.C., chat with residents. Local officials were critical about why it took so long for federal troops to arrive, but when the soldiers finally came, they showed up in force.

BILL FRAKES

A BREATHER

After stopping looters at a Payless Shoe Store, a group of Florida National Guardsmen takes a break. This company, from Homestead, was in a Miami armory when the storm hit, then immediately went into action. It was hours before they were allowed to call home to find out how their families fared.

CHUCK FADELY

115

HELPING HANDS

Marines in Florida City unload supplies from a helicopter. By Thursday, Sept. 3, 10 days after Andrew, federal officials said relief supplies were flowing in smoothly.

JON KRAL

"There have been problems with missed deliveries. There have been problems with long lines."

MICHELLE BAKER, COUNTY DISASTER PLANNER

McRambo

Gary Albert of the Florida National Guard puts a McDonald's character to work, complete with rifle, helmet and a competitor's T-shirt.

AL DIAZ

"The response has been tremendous."

DAVID GIROUX, RED CROSS SPOKESMAN

MEALS TO GO

A U.S. Army field kitchen takes a while to get set up, then serves 300 people hot meals in two hours.

CHARLES TRAINOR JR.

FULL PLATE

Corsha Lee, 5, carries away a lunch at Richmond Heights Middle School, where North Carolina Baptists provided meals for 3,000.

MARICE COHN BAND

READY TO EAT

No one complains about the taste of military rations — at least at first.

BILL FRAKES

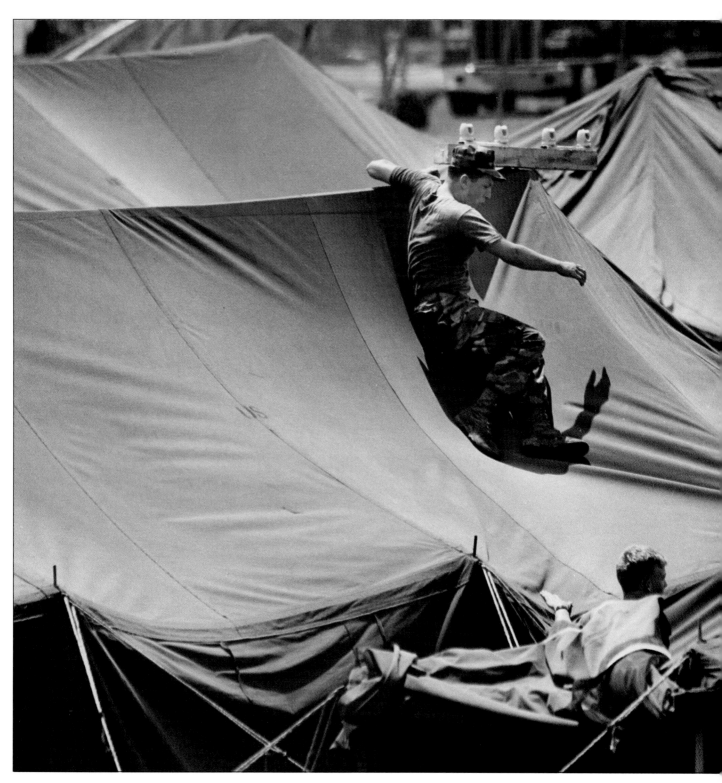

TENTED

In a Homestead park that once was home to barbecues and festivals, U.S. Marines from Camp Lejeune, N.C., set up 108 tents.

CARL JUSTE

NEW CITY

At Harris Field, the orderly row of tents gave the place the look of a military encampment. Many people chose to stay with friends or relatives, and the tents became a home of last resort.

MIKE STOCKER

Aimed Up

In a message directed skyward, a South Dade resident hopes the president looks out the window of Air Force One.

CHUCK FADELY

VISITING

Democratic candidate Bill Clinton first said he didn't want to rush to Dade because it would seem like political opportunism, but several days later, he arrived. In an election year, it was inevitable that the disaster and politics would mix.

AL DIAZ

TENT CITY TOUR

George and Barbara Bush tour the tent city set up at Harris Field in Homestead, during his second visit.

BILL FRAKES

JIM, JENNIE MASHUE

Jim and Jennie Mashue, married 52 years, thought they would live the rest of their lives in retirement bliss at The Villages of Homestead.

A Florida condo with a view to a lake. Close enough to the Homestead Air Force Base so that Jim, a Navy pilot during World War II, could hear the roar of the helicopters. A one-hour drive to Fort Lauderdale, where their son Rick lives. And far, far away from the icy winters of Michigan, where they lived and worked all their lives.

The Mashues moved to the Villages of Homestead six years ago. They bought a second floor two-bedroom condominium for $58,000. They paid cash.

"We thought this was going to be it," Jennie said. "We loved it here. We love taking breakfast in the morning, lunch. With this view of the lake. The sunset. The sand."

Hurricane Andrew changed everything. Now Jim and Jennie are going to be what they had never planned: Gypsies in their old age.

At 72, they are going to

"When I walked in here, I thought, 'Forget it. Total loss.'"

buy a station wagon and tour the country — and visit everybody they know. Renting furnished apartments. Gassing up the tank often.

The day after the hurricane, they drove home from Rick's house.

"Shock," he says. "It was like D-Day."

"State of shock," she says.

The roof was gone over the living room, dining room, breakfast room, bathroom and a TV room. Only the master bedroom and the kitchen survived. The glass cabinets lay atop the bleached wood dining room table. The good china was on the carpet, chipped and dirty.

A foul-smelling mixture of plaster and pink and yellow insulation covered the new navy blue carpet. The walls wet. The furniture ruined. The breeze turning pages

from the scattered books. A blue pillow in the bathtub. Christmas ornaments — green and gold — littered the TV room.

"When I walked in here, I thought, 'Forget it. Total loss,'" Jennie said.

The Mashues are resilient. They've been through worse nightmares, they say. They lost a son 34 years ago. A truck hit his bicycle. Jennie cries a little when she remembers.

Jennie looked over her ruined hat collection. "Nobody wears hats anymore," she says.

They saved the children's pictures. A crystal dolphin with a golden fin. And a gift from one of their sons on their 52nd anniversary: crystal candle holders and a vase. The vase was chipped.

"But the chip won't show once I put flowers in it," Jennie said with a smile.

— MIRTA OJITO

A Deepening Crisis

Heavy rains add to misery of Andrew's victims

WEIGHTED DOWN
A migrant farm worker, Juana Mateo Martinez, moves a heavy sack of clothes, obtained at a relief site, to her van. She lost her home in the storm. After emergency supplies arrived, people began wondering what they were going to do in the long run.

JEFFERY A. SALTER

STRIKING TWICE

On the seventh day after the storm, thunderstorms sweep through South Dade, once again drenching furniture in exposed houses and leaving many people mired in mud. This stark scene, near the Homestead city hall, shows graphically the devastation the city suffered.

JON KRAL

HUGGED

After standing in the rain to get baby diapers at a relief site, this Homestead woman walks away with her child, whom she has protected with a garbage bag.

CHARLES TRAINOR JR.

LOOMING CLOUDS

Jim Case fights to get billowing sheets of plastic down on the badly damaged roof of his uncle's Homestead house before the rains come.

BILL FRAKES

CATCHING DROPS

James Dukes tries to catch some of the rain pouring in through leaks in his roof in Florida City. After Andrew's destruction, even a typical summer afternoon thunderstorm could become a new catastrophe.

C.W. GRIFFIN

WATERLOGGED

Guardsman Todd Bryant talks with Jermain Mitchell, 11, as rain soaks a distribution center in Florida City. After a while, National Guardsmen and Army soldiers become as commonplace as police officers.

CHARLES TRAINOR JR.

LATHERING UP

With water mains broken, people use the canal at Southwest 232nd Street in Goulds as a public bath and swimming hole. After Andrew, necessity became the mother of invention everywhere in South Dade.

JEFFERY A. SALTER

GREENER PASTURES
A family of migrant workers heads out from the Everglades Labor Camp, on the way to Orlando.

C.W. GRIFFIN

As workers cleared the debris, experts started wondering: How many people would move out of the area?

SEARCHING
After going through the rubble searching for the family's immigration papers, a migrant couple picks up a few possessions.

C.W. GRIFFIN

THE NEW ARCHITECTURE

Near their demolished home in the Goldcoaster Mobile Home and RV Park in Homestead, Jack Shaffer and son Ray, 7, build a teepee as wife Shirley watches. Shaffer said he considers himself lucky: He is about to have a two-room household — the teepee and a tent.

JON KRAL

Everywhere, people were learning to make do — and feeling lucky they hadn't lost as much as they could have.

HEADED HOME

After getting food and clothing from the Haitian Mission United Methodist Church, migrant workers head back to their damaged dwellings.

CARL JUSTE

DINING OUT

At the Goldcoaster Trailer Park , a group shares a patio dinner outside a trailer. After the storm, some residents returned to guard their possessions.

JON KRAL

GIVING THANKS

At the flattened Mennonite church in Florida City, Ed Compton (above) searched through the rubble for hymnals. They were then used at an open-air service, led by Pastor Leroy Sheats (at left), standing in front of the remains of the church.

CHARLES TRAINOR JR.

AIR RESCUE

About breakfast time at the Harris Field tent city, three planes spray insecticides to stop mosquitoes. Without windows or electricity, mosquitoes became a huge annoyance in South Dade — and a potential health problem.

JON KRAL

The New Life

Lazaro Sanchez uses a truck mirror to shave at the Harris Field tent city.

C.W. Griffin

Cleaning Up

Alfonso Camargo washes his face at a water stand at Harris Field. The tents are hot, the facilities Spartan.

C.W. Griffin

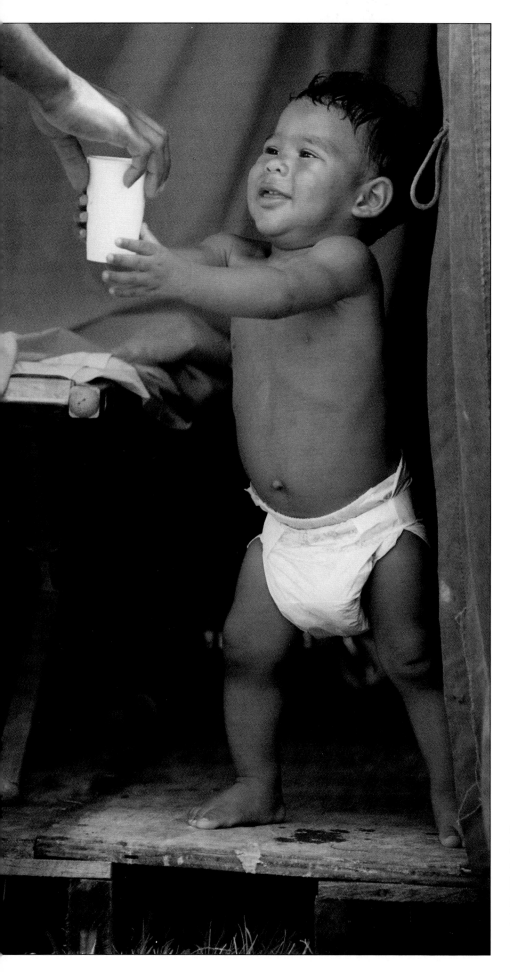

"*It's gonna be rough. I've never lived like this before.*"

BUSTER COLLINS,
MOVING INTO A TENT WITH HIS
WIFE AND THREE CHILDREN

BACK TO BASICS

One-year-old Leo Marshall reaches for a cup of water provided by his dad, Troy, at his new home at Harris Field.

MARICE COHN BAND

COOL TREAT

Rosalind Vicenty, 5, enjoys cooling ice cream at Harris Field. After a few days, people began settling in to the tent city, and federal authorities were uncertain how long the tents would have to remain.

C.W. GRIFFIN

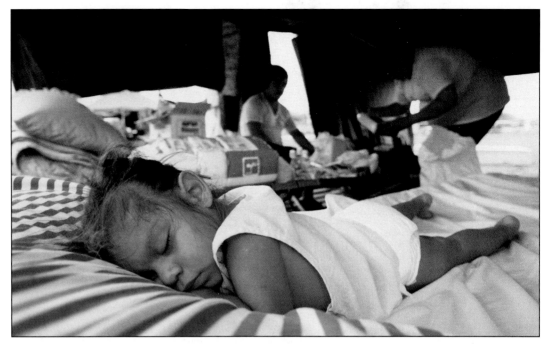

IMPERVIOUS

While her parents settle into their Harris Field tent, Naomi Angela Hernandez, 2, naps on a cot.

MARICE COHN BAND

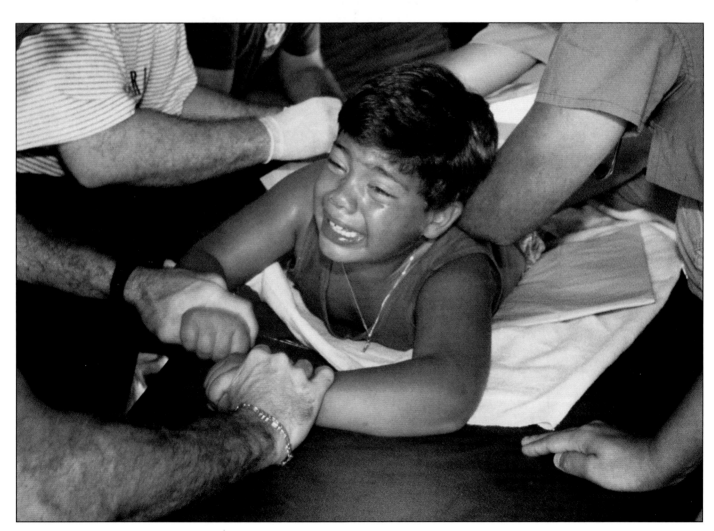

PAINFUL

At a field hospital in Homestead, volunteers hold Emmanuel Sanchez, 7, while a medic sews four stitches to close up a leg wound. Far more people were hurt trying to repair their houses than were injured by the storm itself.

MIKE STOCKER

UNWINDING

Shirley Camargo and Spec. 4 Walter Richter of the 13th Army Band of the North Miami National Guard dance to music being played by other members of the band. Ten days after the storm, people were finally able to relax a little.

C.W. GRIFFIN

MARCIA CHAPPELL

Marcia Chappell's mother, Evelyn Chappell, had a bad feeling that Sunday.

She heard about Andrew at Jackson Memorial Hospital, where she is a nurse. She called Marcia and her pregnant sister Silvia, who lived in Florida City with their seven children. "Come home," she said. "I sense something bad is going to happen."

"And when my Mama got a bad feeling we listen," Marcia, 27, said. "The last time she felt like that my brother was killed. Before he was killed, we were home and she said to us, 'Didn't you hear shots?'"

David Williams, 28, died of five gunshot wounds the next day at Jackson.

The night of the hurricane, the two sisters and their children stayed with their mother in Liberty City.

The next morning, they drove home.

"The closer I got, the sicker I got. I was vomiting," Marcia said. "My sister kept saying, 'Let's go back. Let's go back.'"

The walls were there, but

"Come home," she said. "I sense something bad is going to happen."

the roof and the windows weren't. Their car, inherited from their dead brother, was demolished. The children's new school supplies and clothes were in a puddle of water, plaster and pink insulation material.

And whatever was left in the house, looters had already taken.

With no place to go and afraid to leave the house, the sisters and their children moved into a car — an '85 compact Dodge.

A week later, they moved into a U.S. Marine tent camp a few blocks away.

Andrew made the tough life of Marcia much tougher. Although already poor and partly disabled, she had managed to keep her head above water. To have a roof over her head. To keep her children, Samantha, 6, Maurice, 5, and Ashley, three

months old, fed and healthy.

Now, the tent. Ashley sleeps in a donated crib. The blue and pink bear sheets came in a box, from a stranger. The bottled orange juice and baby food, the soldiers provided.

She has no sense of control. No order in the chaos of her new territory — a few olive green cots and a khaki roof over her head. It sags in the heavy September rains.

Four days ago, her sister had to be hospitalized in the seventh month of her pregnancy. So Marcia will keep her sister's four boys. She gave her two older children to their father in Carol City.

"I hate to split them up," Marcia said, tears quickly forming in the rims of the eyes. "But I have no choice."

— MIRTA OJITO

A LONG HAUL

Expressions of hope for the future, but rebuilding lives and homes will take years

FAST REPAIRS
While friend Johnny Cross offers protection, Charles Johnson hammers nails into the roof of his Homestead home. With so few repairmen available, many people had to do their own work.

CHARLES TRAINOR JR.

QUICK SHOWER
Kathy Harvey washes her 19-month-old son Malkarska in the spray of a broken water main at U.S. 1 and Southwest 172nd Street after a long walk from her Goulds home.

CHARLES TRAINOR JR.

WALKUP SERVICE

Outside State Farm's damaged offices in Naranja Plaza on U.S. 1, agent Tom Ledwidge hands a check for $2,500 to Morris Levy. With the crunch of claims, many homeowners had to wait weeks before an adjuster could give them a final estimate on what their insurance might pay.

C.W. GRIFFIN

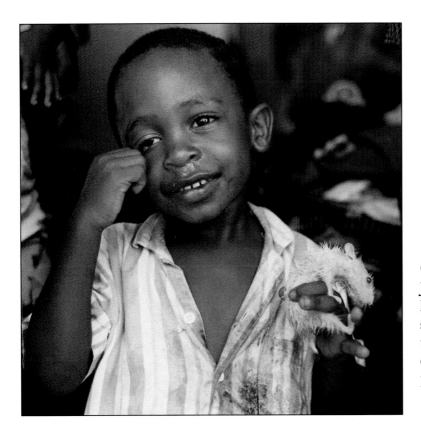

COMFORTED

James Dukes Jr. holds his pet hamster. The soaked hamster survived the storm, but died a couple of days after this photo was taken.

C.W. GRIFFIN

HARD WORK

In West Perrine, Anna Allen, 27-year-old mother of two, takes a break while cleaning up her yard.

JEFFERY A. SALTER

FACING LIFE

The Rev. Jesse Jackson visits South Dade and tells people to stand tough: "It's easy to get blown down the road by a strong tail wind. But your character is measured when you face life's head winds."

MARICE COHN BAND

LABOR OF LOVE

Volunteers from all over help repair the roof of Homestead Church of God in preparation for the next day's services. Many churches were damaged by the storm.

A. ENRIQUE VALENTIN

PAGE 156-157

LONG WAY HOME

Crystal Siwik, 8, walks with her little brother, Eddie, 4, back to the tent where they are staying in Homestead.

JON KRAL

TOMORROW'S ANOTHER DAY

Marjorie Conklin, 40, cools down in a bathtub that her brother dragged from the remains of her mobile home in Florida City. Though residents of the devastated areas knew that it was going to take months, perhaps years, to get their lives back to normal, most people seemed determined not to let Hurricane Andrew get them down.

C.W. GRIFFIN

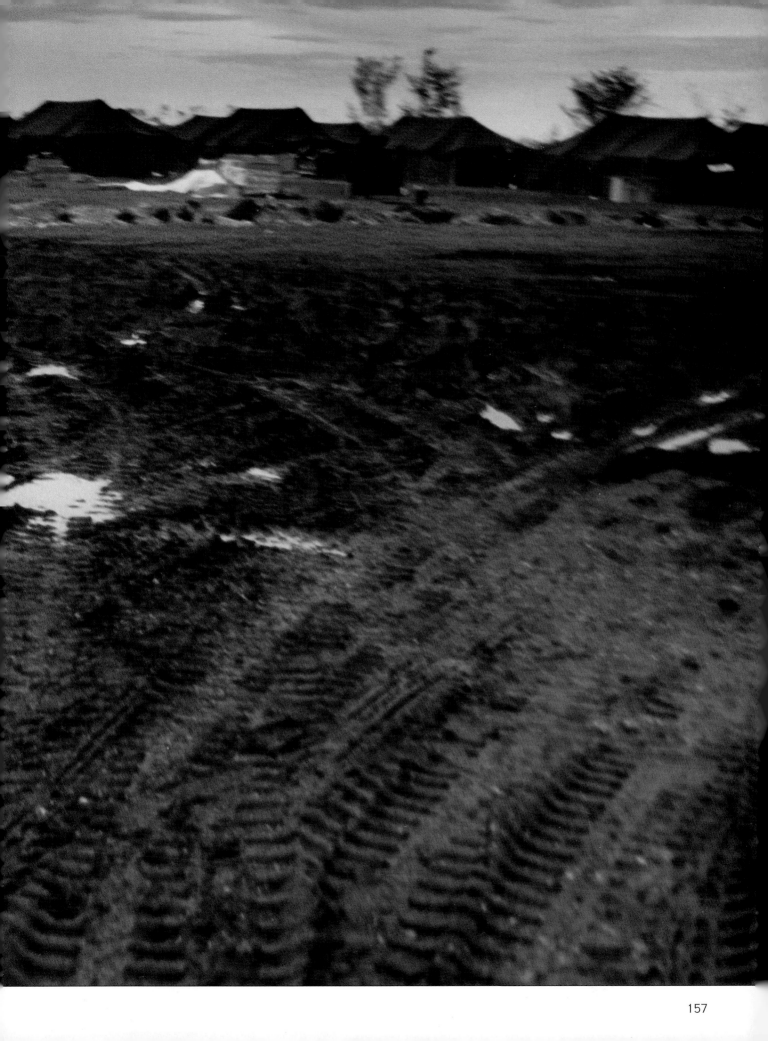

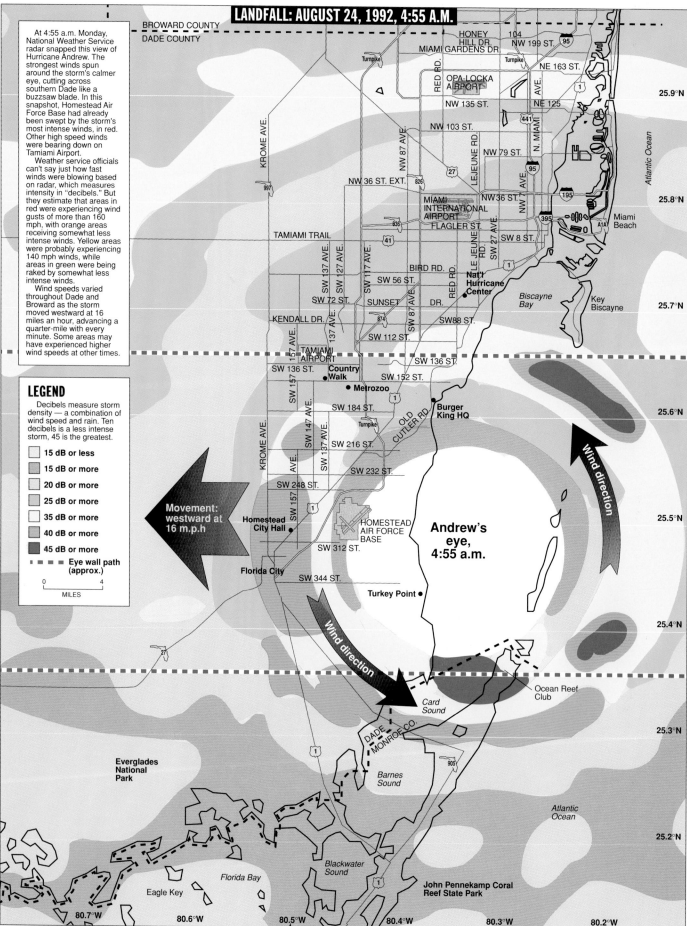

LANDFALL: AUGUST 24, 1992, 4:55 A.M.

BROWARD COUNTY
DADE COUNTY

At 4:55 a.m. Monday, National Weather Service radar snapped this view of Hurricane Andrew. The strongest winds spun around the storm's calmer eye, cutting across southern Dade like a buzzsaw blade. In this snapshot, Homestead Air Force Base had already been swept by the storm's most intense winds, in red. Other high speed winds were bearing down on Tamiami Airport.

Weather service officials can't say just how fast winds were blowing based on radar, which measures intensity in "decibels." But they estimate that areas in red were experiencing wind gusts of more than 160 mph, with orange areas receiving somewhat less intense winds. Yellow areas were probably experiencing 140 mph winds, while areas in green were being raked by somewhat less intense winds.

Wind speeds varied throughout Dade and Broward as the storm moved westward at 16 miles an hour, advancing a quarter-mile with every minute. Some areas may have experienced higher wind speeds at other times.

LEGEND

Decibels measure storm density — a combination of wind speed and rain. Ten decibels is a less intense storm, 45 is the greatest.

- ☐ 15 dB or less
- ☐ 15 dB or more
- ☐ 20 dB or more
- ☐ 25 dB or more
- ☐ 35 dB or more
- ☐ 40 dB or more
- ☐ 45 dB or more
- ▪ ▪ ▪ Eye wall path (approx.)

0 — 4
MILES

Movement: westward at 16 m.p.h

Wind direction

Wind direction

Andrew's eye, 4:55 a.m.

Atlantic Ocean

HONEY HILL DR.
MIAMI GARDENS DR.
OPA-LOCKA AIRPORT
NW 135 ST.
NW 103 ST.
NW 79 ST.
NW 36 ST. EXT.
NW 36 ST.
MIAMI INTERNATIONAL AIRPORT
FLAGLER ST.
TAMIAMI TRAIL
SW 8 ST.
BIRD RD.
SW 56 ST.
SUNSET DR.
SW 72 ST.
KENDALL DR.
SW 88 ST.
SW 112 ST.
TAMIAMI AIRPORT
SW 136 ST.
SW 152 ST.
Country Walk
Metrozoo
SW 184 ST.
SW 216 ST.
SW 232 ST.
SW 248 ST.
Homestead City Hall
SW 312 ST.
Florida City
SW 344 ST.
HOMESTEAD AIR FORCE BASE
Turkey Point

KROME AVE.
NW 87 AVE.
SW 137 AVE.
SW 127 AVE.
SW 117 AVE.
SW 87 AVE.
157 AVE.
137 AVE.
SW 147 AVE.
SW 137 AVE.
LE JEUNE RD.
RED RD.
N. MIAMI AVE.
SW 27 AVE.
OLD CUTLER RD.

Nat'l Hurricane Center
Biscayne Bay
Key Biscayne
Miami Beach

Burger King HQ

Ocean Reef Club

Card Sound

DADE CO.
MONROE CO.

Everglades National Park

Barnes Sound

Blackwater Sound

Eagle Key
Florida Bay

John Pennekamp Coral Reef State Park

Atlantic Ocean

25.9°N
25.8°N
25.7°N
25.6°N
25.5°N
25.4°N
25.3°N
25.2°N

80.7°W   80.6°W   80.5°W   80.4°W   80.3°W   80.2°W

SOURCE: National Hurricane Center, Coral Gables

DAN CLIFFORD / Miami Herald Staff

158

HURRICANE ANDREW'S GRIM TOLL

- 38 deaths in South Florida
- 175,000 homeless in South Florida
- 25,000 homes destroyed; 100,000 damaged
- 1.3 million homes and businesses without power immediately after storm
- 700,000 people evacuated
- 80,000 people housed in shelters
- 7,800 businesses affected, with 120,300 jobs (14% of Dade's economy)
- 22,000 federal troops deployed; largest U.S. military rescue operation ever
- $20 billion in damages
- $10 billion in cleanup costs
- $7.3 billion in insurance claims
- $1.04 billion loss to agriculture

AMONG THE CASUALTIES

IN FLORIDA, MEDICAL EXAMINERS SAID 15 DEATHS WERE DIRECTLY RELATED TO THE STORM; ALL BUT ONE WERE IN DADE COUNTY:

HARRY BOYER, 67
NAOMI BROWNING, 12
HENRY WAYLON BUSH, 41
MARY COWAN, 67
JESSE JAMES, 46
ROBERT MOAK, 32
CLAUDE OWENS, 46
VIDAL PEREZ, 49
GLADYS PORTER, 91
MIGUEL PULIDO, 62
ROBERT RAMOS, 40
ANDREW ROBERTS, 30
NATIVIDAD ROHENA, 57
FRANCISCO SOSPEDRA, 74
THOMAS VANN, 37

TWENTY-THREE DEATHS IN FLORIDA (ALL DADE COUNTY OR NORTH KEY LARGO) WERE INDIRECTLY RELATED TO THE HURRICANE:

ANICE BERETT, 81
JOHN BYERS, 22
JOSE CASTILLO, 36
ALVIA CRUZ, 80
HERBERT ENGLEMAN, 55
EDNA GERRY, 81
JACQUELINE PARKER KOGER, 43
RICHARD KUZINA, 66
HERMAN LUCERNE, 78
FANNIE LYTLE, 94
ANTONIO MACHADO, 52
ANTHONY MARGIOTTA, 79
SHABONNIE MCKENZIE, 9
ALBERTO MIRANDO, 67
EMMA GRACE PARKER, 74
ANTHONY PASTOR, 40
KATHLEEN ROBINSON, 63
MANUEL RODRIGUEZ, 69
JOSE SARAVIA, 73
DOMINIQUE SEYMOUR, 9
FREDERICK STONE, 40
DAGOBERTO TROYA, 50
ELAIDA VARGAS, 22

ACKNOWLEDGMENTS

This book is the culmination of the extraordinary efforts of the 2,600 people who produce The Miami Herald and El Nuevo Herald and the 2,000 who deliver these newspapers to South Florida homes.

THESE ARE THE PEOPLE WHO SPECIFICALLY CONTRIBUTED TO "THE BIG ONE" AND "LA IRA DE LOS VIENTOS," THE SPANISH-LANGUAGE EDITION:

BILL ANDREWS
JOSIE BACALLAO
LINDA BLASH
SHELLY BOWEN
VIC BUBNOW
NANCY COOPER
RAMON DEJESUS
RICHARD DEQUATTRO
ELISABETH DONOVAN
NURI DUCASSI
ED FIOL
DEANNE FORINO
TOM GRALISH, PHILADELPHIA INQUIRER
BILL GREER
BETTY GRUDZINSKI
ED HARDEE
ANDRES HERNANDEZ
ROBERTO HERNANDEZ
OSCAR HERRERA
DAVE HOGERTY
JOSE IGLESIAS
LIZ KLINKENBERG
PETER LAIRD
MAMIE LINGO
JOHN LUKE, DETROIT FREE PRESS
LARRY "BUD" MEYER
LISSETTE NABUT
SUSAN OLDS
ALISON OWEN
LAURA RAUSCH, WICHITA EAGLE
SUSAN A. RODIN
PRISCILLA RODRIGUEZ
CINDY SEIP
STAR SNYDER-PRATHER
RANDY STANO
PATTIE STOKES
AKIRA SUWA, PHILADELPHIA INQUIRER
SAM TERILLI
RICHARD TITLEY, PHILADELPHIA INQUIRER
DENISE TORRES
JOAN TORRIERI
JOHN VAN BEEKUM
BATTLE VAUGHAN
EMMIE VAZQUEZ
PATTY WEINERT

MIAMI HERALD AND EL NUEVO HERALD PHOTOGRAPHERS:

MARICE COHN BAND
CANDACE BARBOT
RANDY BAZEMORE
PETER ANDREW BOSCH
TIM CHAPMAN
ALBERT COYA
AL DIAZ
BOB EIGHMIE
CHUCK FADELY
PATRICK FARRELL
BILL FRAKES
ALAN FREUND
C.W. GRIFFIN
C.M. GUERRERO
A. BRENNAN INNERARITY
CARL JUSTE
BETH A. KEISER
JON KRAL
RICK MCCAWLEY
WALTER MICHOT
DONNA NATALE
MICHELLE PATTERSON
JOHN PINEDA
PETER PORTILLA
JOE RIMKUS JR.
RAUL RUBIERA
JEFFERY A. SALTER
MIKE STOCKER
DEZSO SZURI
CHARLES TRAINOR JR.
A. ENRIQUE VALENTIN
DAVID WALTERS

WITH APPRECIATION FOR THEIR SUPPORT:

BILL BAKER, KNIGHT-RIDDER INC.
JENNIE BUCKNER, KNIGHT-RIDDER INC.
DOUG CLIFTON
GE RENTAL/LEASE
DON KENT, KNIGHT-RIDDER INC.
DAVE LAWRENCE JR.
NORMAN W. SUMMEY COLOR SERVICE
FABIOLA SANTIAGO
ROBERTO SUAREZ
CARLOS VERDECIA
PETE WEITZEL
BILL WILSON, KNIGHT-RIDDER INC.